SHOCK
THE WORLD!

SHOCK
THE WORLD!

A COMPETITOR'S GUIDE
to REALIZING YOUR POTENTIAL

STEVE MELLOR

Cover design by Debraj Dey
Layout by bookmakerfactory.com
Edited by Sean Thomas
Printed in Canada by Gilmore Print Group 10 9 8 7 6 5 4 3 2 1

ISBN 978-1-7777897-7-0

DEDICATION

*For my wife, Britney. My inspiration
to realize my potential.*

SHOCK
THE WORLD

A COMPETITORS GUIDE
TO REALIZING YOUR POTENTIAL

THE STEPS IN THE JOURNEY

⇨ **SHOCK** the Self

⇨ **SHOCK** the Mindset

⇨ **SHOCK** the Approach

⇨ **SHOCK** the Community

⇨ **SHOCK** the Truth

⇨ **SHOCK** the Habits

⇨ **SHOCK** the Resistance

⇨ **SHOCK** the Gap

⇨ **SHOCK** the Execution

⇨ **SHOCK** the World

	Inward Steps	Process Steps	Action Steps
Phase 1	SHOCK THE SELF	SHOCK THE MINDSET	SHOCK THE APPROACH
Phase 2	SHOCK THE COMMUNITY	SHOCK THE TRUTH	SHOCK THE HABITS
Phase 3	SHOCK THE RESISTANCE	SHOCK THE GAP	SHOCK THE EXECUTION

TABLE OF
CONTENTS

PHASE 1

PHASE 2

PHASE 3

INTRODUCTION

How can silence seem so loud? I can hear and feel the adrenaline coursing through my body, and I can't seem to stand still for more than a couple of seconds. Like the thousands of others in the stands, I can sense the magnitude of this moment. But those people don't know how far we've come in just two years. They cannot appreciate how foreign the very idea of this moment was just six months earlier. Yet, amongst the nerves and the anxiety, there is calm, a reassurance, almost a confidence at my core. With the bright lights focused on the finalists, I just sense that the thousands inside this packed, electric arena, and the millions watching from home, were meant to be watching this most unlikely of stories reach its climax.

The silence is broken by the starter saying, "Take your mark," and my nerves resolve into a fierceness laced with expectation. We made this moment; we did not stumble upon it. The plan was always to reach a point where, come race time, we would be 48 seconds from realizing his potential. To go from a complete unknown in the world of swimming to delivering a performance that would place him among the world's elite swimmers. I had done my part and I believed it, which meant I believed he was ready to do his part too. I grin and grab the barrier in front of me with my left hand, where the competitors' coaches' gallery is, and ready my right thumb on the stopwatch.

Bring on the moment, bring on the expectation—it's time to shock the world.

The starter's buzzer sounds. Go!

As soon as the race starts it feels as though he is at the surface swimming. *5.05 to 15 meters. Great first cycle, stroke looks great.* It feels like the 25-meter mark has never come so quickly. *This seems fast.* The watch confirms it as his head passes 25 meters... *Is this too fast?* I wonder as I lean hard into the barrier while tightening my grip on it at the same time. *Is he leading? There is no possible way he's leading the race, right? That was not part of the plan.* The watch confirms his speed yet again: 14.7 seconds as his head passes the 35-meter marker. *We discussed an ideal speed of 15.0 to 35 meters; am I just ahead on the watch?* My hip is now pressing into my hand on the barrier as I'm bent over it at 45 degrees. The clock continues to move along 19, 20, 21. *Here comes the turn, we will get an official check … I'm sure my watch is fast.* 22.56. Second place at the 50-meter mark, one-tenth of a second behind the fastest swimmer on the planet, and right on what my stopwatch says as well.

This is no drill people. We are taking what we came here for… but wait, does the field look like it's a little closer all of a sudden? Is he tiring? 27, 28, 29. Stroke still looks good, I reassure myself, *but I do not like the way swimmers seem to be lining up around him.* 33, 34, 35. My left hand separates from the barrier and finds my head as the stopwatch confirms we are still right where we need to be at the 75-meter mark. 38, 39, 40. And just like that, we enter the final 15 meters. *This is the part we prepared for most,* I reassure myself at my core while my voice bellows, "Reach! Reach! Legs! Legs! …" 43, 44, 45. The watch drops out of my hand but hangs off my wrist as I grab the barrier with both hands and pull myself up to bark out my final orders in the closing 5 meters. "Head down! Head down! HEAD DOWN!" He cannot hear me. He cannot see how close the race is. He has no idea of the magnitude this impending final stroke will have on the finish to the story and this journey we have been on—the future he can write for himself with one last "REACH!!!"

The Reality of the Realization

Realizing potential is one of life's most alluring yet complex processes to take on. While our potential can be seen on the other side of a pane of glass either above or in front of us, we still have to decide if it is worth breaking through the glass to reach it. How thick is that glass? How strong a force must our efforts create to smash it into pieces? Furthermore, our potential can never truly be defined or measured as there are conflicting subjective and objective elements that influence our pursuit of it. You've likely been told about a particular potential you have or you consider yourself as having an untapped potential you have never fully committed to pursuing. But, being aware of your potential is not the same as realizing it. Pursuing your potential stems from a competitive intention to reveal it—to reveal what you are capable of, to reveal your true self, to reveal how much you truly prioritize smashing that metaphorical glass to reach through and realize your potential.

When Brooks Curry realized his potential by becoming a US Olympian in the 100 meters freestyle that night in Omaha, Nebraska, not only did he shock the world of swimming, he completed a two-year process of revealing what he was capable of doing every time he was challenged. Furthermore, I was realizing my potential as a coach, consistently revealing what I could handle and what I could contribute to one athlete's journey to the 2020 Tokyo US Olympic team. As I challenged my ability as a swim coach during this time, I consistently pulled lessons from my own past experiences and from those around me who have excelled in their own competitive worlds.

As the host of the Career Competitor podcast, which I started in June 2018 and continue to host to this day, I have learned from a highly successful and diverse group of professionals from all walks of life. From corporate America, professional sports, entrepreneurship, and many other worlds, champions have shared their journeys with me. My role in these interviews is to identify and explore further the very skills and traits they have relied upon in realizing their potential. After a decade of swim coaching at the highest level, plus the six years prior to that as a world-class athlete myself, and over 100 interviews with competitors and champions, deciphering what made them who they were, I landed on something. The journey I went on with Brooks Curry revealed where my own greatest potential lay and the purpose I had been searching for my entire adult life. Simply put, I realize potential in others.

It was all I had ever known. As an athlete, I believed I had a third of the talent my top competitors in swimming had, so I set out to work three times harder than the guy next to me in pursuit of my potential to become a world-class athlete. My swim coaching career was filled with stories of getting out of athletes what they themselves did not even realize they were capable of. Once they shared their goals with me, it was my responsibility to help them realize what they were capable of, what would be required of them, and to figure out the optimal role I could play in that process.

Today, as a high performance and leadership coach for my company Career Competitor LLC, I guide business owners, leaders, competitors, and teams toward their optimal selves. As you are about to learn in this book, I believe in your optimal self. Yes, you! Whether anyone has ever encouraged you to go after it, whether you have ever believed in it, or whether or not you are aware of the benefits that come with performing as your optimal self, I am excited to introduce you to the *shock the world* mindset. It is best to introduce it as a mindset, although through the course of this book it will become your mission—because I am talking to the competitor within you. To get to executing you must first embody, and I have set this book up in a way to ensure your initial *shock the world* mindset will evolve into the mission I want you to immerse your optimal self in.

Shifting Towards the Optimal Self

The term "optimal self" is something I have marketed and coached over the first year of starting my business. My belief is there is a version of yourself that you aspire to be, one that involves you being your truest self while you pursue your potential. Walking away from a very successful swim coaching career in October of 2021 happened to be the biggest step I had ever taken towards my optimal self. I was only 36 years old and had coached athletes to every international competition across a variety of countries. I had coached multiple male and female swimmers within the NCAA swimming format to All-American status and medal-winning performances within the Southeastern Conference. To then find myself in Omaha, Nebraska days after having put Louisiana State University's first-ever swimmer onto a US Olympic team wondering if this career was for me—something didn't quite add up.

In the world of swim coaching, I was very much at the top of the mountain at this moment, and very little about it felt like I thought it would. Sure, I was incredibly proud; not only had I just helped facilitate the most unlikely of Olympic berths, but it was done with no shortage of challenges and very little support from outside the bubble we kept ourselves in. But outside of the pride, I felt a sense of not relating to my new peers who were more established at the pinnacle of the sport. Was something wrong with me? Not only did I not relate to the notion of being an Olympic swim coach, but I also found myself questioning if I even saw myself as a swim coach.

I did not live and breathe the sport like many of my peers. It is one of the things I cherished working for my boss Dave Geyer for 10 years: I could be myself; I could learn as myself; I could fail as myself; and I could coach as myself. Away from the pool, I often thought about athletes and how to get more out of them, but I did not care to follow the sport or read up on it to advance my knowledge in any way. In the days after Brooks qualified for the US Olympic team, I was inundated with questions from fellow coaches regarding his training plan and special swim sets he might have done to become the elite swimmer he was. I would always answer with details of the evolution of Brooks the *person*, what we had built within him to optimize what we got out of him. And, I would always highlight the time invested in our relationship as well. But Brooks just happened to be the first US Olympian I had coached, which is why people suddenly had questions. *This is how I have always coached*, I thought.

My coaching philosophy was always "meet the person where they are." For some that might mean making an Olympic team; for others, it might be swimming a best time for the first time in three years. The spectrum is wide and filled with a variety of goals and intentions for an athlete's swimming career. When working with any athlete, my initial plan was always to help them first understand what would be required to reach goals, and then get to work on realizing this potential they saw in themselves. And, there in Omaha, as I reflected on my many, many experiences of doing exactly this over the past 10 years of swim coaching, it hit me. I had never been a swim coach this entire time: I had been a coach of swimmers. The world I had existed in was swimming, and I was helping swimmers realize their potential, but, I did it by coaching them, the person. If you can help grow and develop the competitor within a specific world, you can make them a success and, in time, a champion. This whole time, even though I understood and could apply the physical work required to help swimmers swim faster, at my core I had been focused mainly on realizing people's potential. They got to decide the world they wanted to shock and were capable of shocking. I was there to help make it happen.

KNOW THE WORLD

The focus of this book is the world as *you* know it. Each and every one of you must consider the "world" you plan to shock in the process of realizing your potential. It can be a specific field or industry that you've been a part of and flown under the radar so far, or it can be one you have yet to introduce yourself to. It can be a group of people or a particular demographic that, history shows, either do not believe in your potential or they just don't know who you are. It can be as personal as the world you live within today, or it can be *the* world—the whole world, and nothing less. Because depending on who you are and what you believe you're capable of accomplishing, there might just be a chance to send shockwaves around the planet. It is, however, vital that you know precisely the world you plan to shock for this book to serve the purpose it sets out to do. We will examine that world at times, along with the people within it, and the gaps between that world and where we find ourselves currently.

THE JOURNEY AHEAD

With the world you will come to shock in mind, I want to familiarize you with the layout of what you are about to cover across the 10 chapters. Aside from chapter 10, you will gain various insight on implementing steps known as shocks that impact one of the three areas that I believe make up any competitor's journey to realizing potential:

- How you impact your internal growth

- How you impact your process

- How you impact the actions you take

Chapters 1, 4, and 7 will focus on impacting internal growth, with chapters 2, 5, and 8 impacting your process, while chapters 3, 6, and 9 will impact the actions you take. By the time we reach chapter 10, you will feel prepared to shock the world, you will see how you can shock the world, and you will be compelled to go out and shock the world.

Let this become your mantra as it did for Brooks Curry and me. The moment I presented the notion of making the US Olympic team to Brooks in my office back in August 2019, I looked him in the eye and declared, "Let's go shock the world." It became our way of reinforcing the size of the task at hand. Every bit of progress we felt, every success achieved, adversity encountered, or recalibration made along the way, we would reaffirm our mission. It would be the seal on a discussion or an action taken: "Shock the world, brother." "Shock the world, coach." It was our way of acknowledging the task at hand and keeping it always at the forefront of our minds.

As you start this book, you have a choice in terms of the perspective you read it from: the perspective of someone implementing it themselves, or someone who will try to lead others to realize their potential. It is why the book is in three phases, because, no matter if you are realizing your own potential or facilitating the process in others, you must respect the order the information is presented – especially if you are leading others to realize their potential. You cannot expect to focus on a person's habits, resistance, or execution if you are not willing to invest in their self and their mindset. There is a formula here that must be respected and considered, and it will serve you well in time, even if it takes a little longer to do.

But, before you start, let me address this important point one last time. I believe in your potential. Need me to say it again? I BELIEVE IN YOUR POTENTIAL! I believe you have what it takes to embrace and incorporate the messages I'm about to impart to you. While I like to present content as simply as possible, a simple notion does not equate to easy application. You may need to re-read parts of this book at times to comprehend fully what is being asked of you. You will likely come back to a part of the book once you start to follow through on the steps presented there and need a refresher. Most importantly, you will have the chance to make this book your own. Do not just think about what I present and challenge you with; write those thoughts down on the page. Make this book your own from here on out. Leave nothing to chance. Know that as you work through one section you are putting down thoughts that you can reference and later build upon as you progress.

I have great admiration for you at this early stage because, at this moment, by starting the journey, you are believing you are capable of more. That mindset will take you far. It will drive you in becoming your optimal self. It will be the springboard to go *shock the world*.

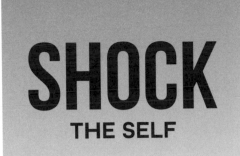

SHOCK
THE SELF

INWARD STEP

How did we get here? No this isn't a biology book about the birds and the bees. I'm talking about how did we end up in this place on our journey, feeling compelled or incentivized to discover what will be required to "shock the world." Not to be the bearer of bad news, but it is important to take a step or two back before striving forward towards anything. You see, this book is lined throughout with deliberate acts. Nothing is left to chance, or to hoping and wishing. Chances are you can pinpoint a few people who have gotten to where they are today thanks to a host of timely factors going their way. But for the sake of this book, let us assume lady luck isn't planning to show up. You will be the driver and the navigator, and you will take on a host of other responsibilities to get you to your destination. As you comprehend the amount of time you will be spending with yourself, you must truly know who this person is that will be doing all the work.

As I write, I hope this book finds you in a wonderful place in your life. Happy with what you have accomplished and excited about the future. Although it is possible that things are only okay and have been a little stagnant of late. It is even possible that you are reading this while dealing with a number of setbacks and you feel quite pessimistic about the future. Chances are, you have experienced all of these scenarios at different junctures of life and felt your sense of self challenged. When things are going well, we can be guilty of making assumptions about who we are. Then hardships that come our way leave us susceptible to harsh inner talk, where we dismiss parts of ourselves that we may have once admired. When we don't have a firm grasp of who we are, the rollercoaster of life can throw us out of the car so often that we never get to know the person who keeps climbing back on board.

Losing Yourself in Transition

From my own personal experience of retiring as an athlete and having seen hundreds of others do the same, transitions might just be the chapters of our lives where a person's identity is challenged most. It is almost as though we lose ourselves in the transition, looking at where we came from and where we are going, a spotlight ushering us forwards while we can't remember asking for a spotlight at all. And, back in 2018, when I started out on my podcasting journey, I welcomed the ideal first guest to validate how our identity can seem like the last of our concerns—until it becomes the absolute concern.

Raymond De Padua was a member of the men's team during my first year as a swim coach at LSU back in 2011. I never worked with him directly but we built a rapport based simply on the fact that he was down to earth, easy to talk to, and liked to initiate discussions with me about optimal performance. Then I watched his life evolve over the first 4–5 years after graduating as he bounced around many different careers with a willingness to grind and prove himself. But as he mentions in the episode, while performing at high standards through self-inflicted 60-hour work weeks, he hated what he was doing and resented himself for it.

It is understandable for a competitive person to want to be associated with those at the top of their game, but what Raymond didn't consider was who he would have to be in order to be a part of that. He admits he was attracted by the notion of telling people he worked for industry leaders, people who set the standards for excellence; but he had yet to realize he yearned to prove it was he who could set the standard for excellence within an industry. Ray eventually realized that he was an entrepreneur thanks to surrounding himself with people able to help him see himself for who he was. A simple reconnection with a couple of old friends from the swimming world provided the catalyst he needed to commit to his best self. The competitive, creative, and ambitious Ray that had always been there finally sensed how he could optimize his performance: by being his truest self.

By the time Ray and I spoke in June of 2018, he was well on his way into entrepreneurship and had a lot of different balls that he was juggling. Another four years later, the demands are greater and the number of balls continues to increase. Today he has two thriving companies in Prints R Us and Local Retreats, where he is responsible for $100 million in assets and over forty employees. It doesn't bother him that he is busier than ever because "you never work a day in your life when you do something that you love." Now, as cliché as this old saying might be, to build this perspective Ray had to work on who he was at his core; he had to learn to love himself before he could even contemplate doing what he loved for a living.

As with any loving relationship in our lives, regular and recurring work is required in order to maintain the quality at the heart of self-love. It is important to prioritize knowing ourselves inside and out, and sometimes that is not possible to do alone. In Ray's case, he started to progress towards the life he has today when others helped him see his truest self. How can others do that for you?

Realization Exercise

⇨ Who in your life knows you best? _____

⇨ What can they tell you about yourself that maybe you wouldn't notice or value?

I am now aware of the following qualities about myself I had yet to consider:

_____ , _____ , _____

THE HARSH REALITY

Having someone close to you identify qualities that make you the person they admire and love is a great way to set the wheels in motion for the difficult work ahead in this first chapter. It is essential to understand fully who you are before taking on any more steps towards revealing your potential. I want you to focus inwardly and ask yourself the most difficult question known to mankind: Who are you? Go ahead, ask yourself that—today, please—because I would hate for you to wait as late as I did to ask myself that very same question.

It was the summer of 2012. At that time, I had been in the United States for seven years after arriving from England in 2005. I was a master's degree graduate from North Carolina State University and a year into my first full-time job as a collegiate swim coach at Louisiana State University. More pressingly, I'd been waiting to hear for most of the past six months about the status of my next visa to continue working in the US. But I'd been doing some great things already in my young career, and things were truly going well. I was making impact, shifting the culture. The athletes had truly bought into me, and I was looking at a long and successful future in the profession. Then: Visa denied. Wait, what? That couldn't be right.

Denied.

Yes, that's what it said. It didn't make sense. People in the athletic department who didn't have any expertise on this matter told me they would get it sorted out. The sweet lady in international services, with zero qualifications on immigration law, had said she was pretty sure it would go through. I couldn't believe she had misjudged that after telling me for five months we should have an answer in a matter of weeks. Sarcasm aside, I had no option but to return to the United Kingdom.

It was literally that simple. Go back to where it all began and give up my American dream. The problem was, I had nothing. A small amount of savings, a car with 200,000 miles on it, no network or job leads in the UK, and an apartment filled with belongings I'd quickly need to find storage for. For six weeks back in England, while communicating back-and-forth with LSU hoping they might figure something out, it was me, myself, and I in my childhood bedroom wondering where it had all gone wrong.

Turns out I didn't really like the guy I was forced to spend time with over those six weeks. I was a lost cause. I had no plan or vision for the future. I didn't see the world in a particularly good light. And wow, did I hate myself. I mean, I despised myself. I thought I offered nothing to the world and just wanted things to get resolved in the hope that it would distract me from the fact I hated myself. After six weeks of self-loathing, I used what little money I had left and flew back to the US to tie up all the loose ends, say goodbye to friends I had made over seven years of being there, and sell my belongings. Picture the scene. The contents of my entire apartment laid out on my boss's driveway, while I accept strangers' offers of next to nothing for my last remaining possessions because I literally had to get rid of them. I will never forget that day. I was forced to face my terrible circumstances in life, while addressing and accepting that I hated the person I had become. I had hit rock bottom, desperately looking for a way out.

Establishing an Identity

A person's identity is a distinguishing character or personality of an individual. A person's mindset is a mental attitude or inclination. The two deserve a seat at the table. On one side there is a person that we spend a lot of time with internally that most days people will get glimpses of. While on the other side we have the calling card version of ourselves that is delivered in order to perform to standards expected of us.

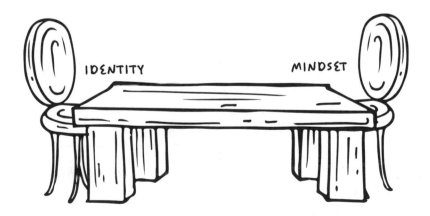

They live in the same space and occupy a great deal of our thoughts, behaviors, and actions. For us to be successful we must get very comfortable with both, embrace them, figure each one out, and establish how they will serve our journey towards shocking our world. Understand this: they are different, separate entities, and they must be treated as such. This is not a case where one ends and the other takes its place; we are talking about two seats, two stations, two roles, but both equally vital and impactful.

I personally regard having a sense of self as being familiar with one's identity, which is why familiarizing ourselves with our identity is the focus of this chapter. In order to *shock the self*, we must start by revealing what we currently know about it. What is there to know? What is there to like? What is there to avoid? I have to assume that if you are looking to shock the world, then you must love what it is you do (quick tip: if this is not the case, this book is going to be an uphill climb for you). The important part of loving what you do is firstly loving yourself. Not just having a good idea of who you are or having a good feel for how you work—I mean feeling strongly enough about yourself that you feel the need to celebrate who you are. So, if you have even an ounce of hesitation about being completely in love with who it is you are, consider this exercise.

Let's return to my million-dollar question: Who are you? Let's take some time to identify who you are at your best, and who you are at your worst, which can be a difficult list to create without some prompting. When analyzing my story of having to start over in the UK, I was losing parts of my life where I loved myself, and inheriting moments where I did not love myself. I was revealing key parts of my identity that I loved and did not love, and if you reflect on the highs and lows of your journey, I am sure you will be able to see your best and worst traits in there too.

Realization Exercise

	When I enjoy what I am doing	When I do not enjoy what I am doing
Things I love about myself		
Things I do not love about myself		

You should be starting to visualize what you love and do not love about yourself across most situations, with the intention being to love all parts of you by the end of this chapter, no matter the situation. We have to shift our mindset towards appreciating all we bring to our whole day, every day. If we have any hope to shock the world one day, then we better get used to loving and embracing the good, the bad, and the ugly about ourselves. We need to have the ability to check in and remind ourselves that we are doing what we love, and not just during the tough times in order to keep us going. It can be implemented as a celebratory tool. It's important that, in time, you establish a love for yourself and a love for what you do, and I believe it should happen in that order. Furthermore, this love can grow into a personal standard for what you are and are not willing to do.

FIND YOUR NORTH STAR

Soon after my depressing garage sale, I left American soil and headed back to the UK where I would be starting a job in recruitment. This was a mistake. Nothing against the recruiting game, but the decision to work in this field hit me while I was down following the abrupt relocation back home. But the hit also rattled me into action and started me on a four-year climb to learning to love myself. Recruiting was never going to be something I'd love to do and I would never love myself doing it. Again, nothing against those who do it; in fact, two of my closest friends have made amazing careers for themselves in it. The fact was that, at that time, it just didn't bring my best self to the surface. But doing something so different (I was recruiting for people in the mining industry, which might just be the exact opposite of swim coaching) made me realize the parts that I loved about what I was previously doing. I loved coaching, and I always had. I missed building meaningful and purposeful relationships on a shared ambition to optimize performance. I missed collaboratively making and chasing goals, ones that were emotionally driven and the kind of value to someone that money could not buy.

I won't bore you with the details of my climb back up from rock bottom (spoiler alert: I made it!). What provided my north star throughout that time was ensuring I pursued a path that honored the best version of myself. Remaining loyal to the pursuit of your best self allows you to familiarize yourself with, and embrace, the competitor that you are. To love something is to be honest towards it, to give your entire self to it as we do in our most committed relationships. Now is the time to commit fully to honoring your best self and the competitor you are. Your plan to shock the world cannot come at the expense of you. So, make that agreement now, to love and honor yourself throughout this journey, and visualize that version of you—and only that version—realizing your potential.

Respectfully Finding a Place for Yourself

As you start to envision your best self shocking the world, now is the time to paint a clearer picture of that world. What makes it the world it is? Do you see yourself within it? What does the path to success within this world look like? What characteristics do successful people within it embody? It is important to be able to answer these questions in great detail because the last thing we want to happen is for you to be left shocked by the world you were intending to shock. Investing all this time in ourselves to end up with egg on our faces is not the goal of this book, so let's look at this essential step properly.

Meet Shikha Uberoi Bajpai, a guest of mine on the Career Competitor podcast. Shikha is a fierce, Indian woman who has made a life and career for herself by shocking worlds that historically are not populated by her Indian people. This former world top 200-ranked tennis player also had dreams of getting behind the camera and creating media content within her culture that may challenge traditions. But she knew her culture; she held it so dearly to her heart that despite pursuing an unpopular sport and career, she would always honor her best self and culture. She created documentaries and reality TV shows during a time in India where this was not part of mainstream media. This former world-class athlete was now using her platform, network, and education (as a graduate of Yale) to catapult herself into the mainstream and shock the Indian culture by exposing it to a new brand of media. It was all very well received and even celebrated in time, making Shikha a trailblazer for media movements within Indian culture.

None of this was reckless, none of this was without intent, and all of it stood to shock the world within which she was operating. Shikha saw so much of herself within the Indian culture but felt she could realize her best and competitive self respectfully while challenging traditions both in sports and culture. Today, Shikha is President of Indi, a company empowering hundreds of thousands of individuals to cash in on their passions through content creation. What better person to be in a leadership role in this company than a woman who successfully created impactful content within a world that did not even know they could benefit from it.

As you look at yourself and then look at the world you plan to shock, where do you see yourself? Do you see success stories around you that come from your background, that look like you, resemble your character, and that offer what you offer? Whose approach mirrors what you consider yours to be? In Shikha's case, while striving to impact Indian culture she could lean on examples from media worlds elsewhere. She was not reinventing the wheel, but she was pushing barriers and breaking through ceilings to shock the world that she knew best.

Realization Exercise

Who are three people in your world that you want to either emulate or surpass?

_____ , _____ , _____

What traits within you do you believe these people embody?

SHOW UP AS THE ONE YOU LOVE

Some of you might be looking at achieving something that no person has ever done before, and if that is you, I am delighted, because you chose the ideal book to get you there. But to start, the world you plan to shock must show signs that a person like you—the self that you are learning to love—has a part to play in this world. Remember, we are not *creating* a world to shock (later we will discuss creating a community, but that's different), we are shocking an already established world.

Answering the big question of "who are you?" should not scare you as much as it should challenge you. It should become a question you relish answering as you become clearer about your truest sense of self and why you love that person. You are familiarizing yourself with the person that you are, whom you love, and are so excited to see this person realize their potential. Over the course of forthcoming chapters, you will continue to gain a stronger grasp of who you are and what that person is truly capable of. But, for the time being, let's move on and address that other, equally important, seat at the table I mentioned earlier. The mental attitude of the competitor we need to show up. Our mindset.

You are ready to Shock the Self because

⇨ You have identified and will continue to identify what you love about yourself.

⇨ You have identified what you don't love, but will learn to love about yourself.

⇨ You recognize what you love about yourself in those you strive to emulate and surpass.

Your identity will be best known for these 5 things:

Why we should Shock the Self

Love you 〉 Love representing you 〉 Love working for you 〉 Love what you do

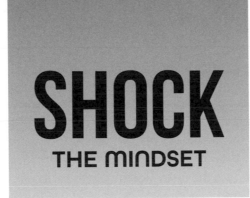

SHOCK
THE MINDSET

There appears to be a climate these days where we are coerced into extreme reactions. Statements made and questions asked spark outrage, abandonment, condemnation, or some other extreme reaction. Anyone who has worked within an office or larger organization will likely have witnessed the negative communication and accusations associated with such reactionary cultures. Members of staff reacting to events within their professional world, coerced into conversations devoid of productive value; just reacting, just venting, with little to no intention behind what's being said. At the roots of falling victim to joining in such conversations are the same natural tendencies when encountering traffic on the road. We get pulled in by the frustration and are guilty of adding to it, finding ourselves fueled by rage towards situations and the decisions of others that tend to be out of our control.

While the example above describes a typical scenario, let's now focus specifically on the world you are planning to shock. In what ways does this world prompt a reaction from you? Do you trust your response when encountering a disagreement? What areas frequently trigger a reaction from you? In my world of coaching, I have learned over the years to gain control over my reactions to what athletes or clients of mine present to me. The last thing I want to be responsible for is fueling a destructive mindset. The more I can absorb the reactions of those I coach before responding to them, the more beneficial my response will be.

YOUR GREATEST VOICE

As a reader of this book, I consider you a client – someone likely having an internal response to what I am writing, that I hope sparks a fire within you to act. But I want you to absorb this information and formulate your response without allowing your body to just drive an immediate response. Our body is the first voice that speaks to us, and we have the ability to either listen to it, or allow it to lead our immediate response. One of my favorite things to tell clients is how our bodies are our greatest voice. We must build a relationship with our body where we learn how best to respond to it, build a trust for it, and truly grasp how it is either guiding us effectively or leading us to a place we may regret.

Champion athletes know the benefits of an optimal relationship with their body to guide the process. Three-time Olympic gold medalist Tianna Bartoletta has shaped an inner voice to guide her towards becoming a champion; first, through learning to love herself before developing the mindset to perform against the best. In our discussion, Tianna presented the notion of "following the rabbit down the hole," which is an exploratory process to better understand her physical and emotional reaction to a result or an event. This routine of familiarization advances her mindset and sense of self each time and helps paint a picture of her potential optimal self (a reoccurring theme on the pod—you will be a listener by the end of this book, I just know it!). She emphasized the need to embed within ourselves a commitment to "leave no stone unturned" when seeking clarification for why our mind and body responds the way it does.

This approach presented here by Tianna pertains to all of us, not just an elite athlete. Like you, Tianna is a competitor, driven towards optimizing herself in order to optimize the athlete she wants to be. It starts with her—the person, not the athlete—as she repeatedly emphasized in our discussion. Her investment in herself fueled her mindset towards how she lived and showed up each and every day as an elite athlete. That consistent approach to how she listens to her body has led to a trust and foundation for how she reacts and responds as an athlete. Whatever the world you are currently in or planning to compete within, it would serve you well to listen to what your body is saying and develop trust for how it can serve you moving forward.

Realization Exercise

Consider a recent extreme reaction you dealt with. Follow the rabbit down the hole with how you could optimize your response.

1. How do I recall my body responding in this reactive moment?

2. What can I learn about myself based on how my body responded?

3. What about this discovery is something I have control over?

4. How can I better control this controllable moving forward?

5. What other scenarios tend to prompt this type of initial reaction?

The Evolution of Control

Dedicating time for going down rabbit holes and assessing how you respond and react to certain situations develops a mindset capable of absorbing the significance of what is happening. It allows you to become poised and much more present in moments as opposed to allowing specific moments to control you. While this is a great way to shock the mindset towards realizing your potential, few of us get to this point without starting where I did in my coaching career.

I was pure emotion, likely overreacting and incorrectly responding every moment I was coaching. My world had total influence over my reactions, and it was preventing me from seeing the whole picture when it came to an athlete's development. If an athlete misunderstood my directions, I would hammer them with questions about why they were not listening, not once considering that maybe I didn't present the information clearly enough. Afterward, when an athlete performed below my expectations, I would want answers, never considering that perhaps my expectations were unrealistic or that they might not have been shared prior to the performance.

I was a young, cocky, over-ambitious 26-year-old who thought he had it all figured out. But, time has taught me on my coaching journey (and life journey for that matter) a very clear reality: our world is filled with influences and decisions beyond our control. How we respond to them, however, is one of the few things we actually *can* control. The podcast has exposed me to many tales of competitors realizing the power that comes with *controlling the controllables;* but I do not believe this is a skill that can ever be perfected. We all have that person, scenario, or attitude that prompts a reaction we cannot control. While such moments are prone to crop up during a typical day (I hope to get a handle on my road rage one of these days), we cannot afford to let the uncontrollable moments within the world we are targeting to have detrimental effects.

Something as simple as how we start a sentence can demonstrate the difference between an out-of-control and controlled mindset. Instead of responding to a disappointing realization with "I hate when…," we could instead say, "It appears as though…." Such a small difference, yet one that will shift entirely how you react, because an initial thought sets up the thoughts that follow.

Example

Event:
A prospective client or customer is late and has not communicated why.

Ineffective Response:
"I hate when people just don't let you know they're running late. It is so inconsiderate. They clearly don't respect my time or me for that matter. Why I am even bothering with this?"

Effective Response:

"It appears as though they are running late. They must have gotten delayed somehow. But I can use however long I have to prep more. This is an opportunity to be even more ready for them."

If you respect what your world demands of those seeking success, you will ensure you shape your mindset accordingly to bring the best version of yourself into it. To realize your potential, your mindset has to become the attitude your world demands of you. Your inclination must be to respond to what your world presents you in a way that preserves the chance to realize your potential. There is too much at stake to succumb to the negative influences your world can have on you by getting distracted from your intentions. You know by now that you are showing up to do what you love to the best of your ability, so your mindset must be a combination of traits and qualities to allow your best self to flourish. Simply put: you have learned to love yourself, now build a mindset capable of protecting this version of yourself.

SEIZE THE OPPORTUNITY TO SMASH THROUGH

Glass ceilings have provided many a limitation throughout history to potentially discourage the most capable of competitors from even trying—entire demographics wanting to succeed in a world that historically favors those much more established and proven not to be accepting of others. If you relate to dealing with such obstacles, you will probably need to embody qualities that do not deter you if you are ignored or rejected. In this example, a competitor would want to incorporate resiliency, outgoingness, assertiveness, composure, and assurance within their mindset, just to name a few. Such qualities would strengthen you to show up and handle rejection, capitalize on opportunities to connect with people, and to learn from any and all encounters.

The history of women in sports is an example of how powerful mindsets have overcome a pervasive lack of opportunity and representation. I spoke with Elizabeth Benn on my podcast who, as I write this book, has been appointed the Director for Major League operations with the New York Mets. This title made her the highest-ranking female baseball operations employee in franchise history and part of a special group of women willing to pursue a career in a highly male-populated industry. Elizabeth's story personifies what it means to, firstly, honor and implement an identity, as she pursued her life's passion of baseball growing up in Canada. In turn, remaining true to her identity led her to opportunities where she could see herself having a future in the game (i.e., in the world of baseball), but understood the mindset required to make this a reality.

Right or wrong, the fact was, Elizabeth had to demonstrate a level of interest in and knowledge of the game that rivaled—and even surpassed—men working in the industry. She had to be willing to get involved and even play the sport with men to gain the respect required (again, right or wrong) for them to trust her judgment. And when she was able to get work experience, she had to show up daily knowing she might not be given the same treatment as her male counterparts. Furthermore, she had to remain conscientious of her reactions to potential adversities in order to optimize her career development and realize her goals.

Women have been smashing through glass ceilings across all industries for decades thanks in part to how they have dealt with the worlds they've worked within. When they've encountered narrow-mindedness or a misogynistic supervisor, they've figured out how best to react. If they felt they were overlooked for promotions because they weren't permitted to be part of the boy's club, they once again found the best and most appropriate way to react. It should without saying that these scenarios should never have occurred; but they have been the reality, and women the world over have dealt with them for centuries. Yet, despite such hardships, women everywhere have managed to send shockwaves through their worlds thanks to a mindset built on overcoming barriers.

Realization Exercise

What limiting factors exist for you in the world you plan to shock?

Consider demographic, education, experience, history, everything.

What must your mindset embody in order to overcome such factors?

These must be traits that people can see you embodying (e.g., assertiveness)

Why are you capable of embodying this mindset?

Revert back to what you love about yourself and how your mindset can be shaped by these things.

NEVER STOP LISTENING AND LEARNING

Back to the role our body plays in this – listen to what it is telling you. Dedicate time to exploring yourself and shaping your mindset, but continue doing this as you take initial steps towards what it is you are doing in your world. Consider when you first start networking with other people in your chosen world. While some people thrive, others ... well, let's just say it is not for everyone. But the opportunity presents itself almost daily in a variety of ways. The obvious scenario is, of course, being at a networking event; but there are many less obvious ones, like when you're grabbing a coffee and the person next to you starts chatting to you about what you do. In both scenarios, what is your body telling you? Do you find yourself excited to talk or is your body sweating and irritable because of the interaction? Do you find yourself leaning into the person with intent or turning away with annoyance or embarrassment? Your body is constantly talking to you, and like your mindset, you have to get to know it, analyze it, and gain some sort of control over it.

The more we listen to our body, the more we know when to listen to it, but also when to ignore it. For instance, if someone is engaging in conversation that could be of benefit to you, and you are maybe feeling embarrassed, ignore the urge to remove yourself. Rather, whenever such difficult encounters occur, reflect on them and ask why your body responded and spoke to you the way it did. What are you embarrassed about? What about your mindset must shift in order to relish such moments in the future? These reflective acts are so powerful because they are seeds of growth.

Before you start wondering if I am asking you to change who you are, I am not. I am only starting you off on the road to loving yourself and embracing who you truly are. The last thing I want is for you to ignore that identity. You must see your mindset as an extension of yourself, the competitive representation required to shock the world. But that is enough private, behind the scenes work for now. It's time to take our first step towards action.

You are ready to Shock the Mindset because

⇨ You understand the value of listening to your body when it talks.

⇨ You see what your world demands of those who have been successful.

⇨ You know how to absorb what is happening as opposed to reacting to it.

Your mindset will be best known for these 5 things:

Why we should Shock the Mindset

Shape your Mindset ⟩ Shape your Impact ⟩ Shape your Response ⟩ Shape your Future

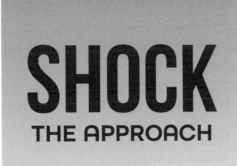

SHOCK
THE APPROACH

ACTION STEP

My wife and I got engaged after six months of dating. We were both in our very early thirties, neither had ever been engaged, but we had both spent years in unsuccessful relationships. One afternoon while my wife (girlfriend at the time) was away at a work conference, I was laying on my couch thinking of her. I had been pondering the idea of marrying this girl I was crazy about for the past couple weeks. Then, suddenly I just hopped up off the couch, grabbed my car keys, and went to go buy a ring. Interestingly, just eight months earlier I had started therapy to work on me and my identity because I really didn't know or trust who I was when I had turned 30. Because of that, my mindset towards dating was filled with doubt, fogginess, pessimism, all of which was centered on me mainly. I did not like all of myself, which made the idea of loving and committing to another person very difficult. To then meet this woman a matter of weeks into therapy, was a God-given opportunity to establish the very world I had dreamt of while growing up—being happily married, having a beautiful family—and it was an opportunity I could not waste. I was learning to love myself through therapy. I was working daily on the mindset required to be in a loving and committed relationship. What was I waiting for? This woman was the world I had always wanted, so why remain quiet? Why not announce my intentions to have this life? Thank God she said yes.

When you coach as long as I have, you lose track of how much "talk" you've heard from people unwilling to support their words with action. Now, with an improving grasp of your identity and the shaping of the mindset you will need to shock the world, it is time to lead with action. To reassure you, we are not currently performing with a lot at stake. No, this is more about stepping out of the shadows and into the light for the first time. I did not write this book to create a line of cocky individuals that think by spending time working on themselves, they now have it all figured out. The work so far demonstrates our willingness to know ourselves and have the humility to accept what will be required. An empowering part of what was required to get to this point is that you have qualified yourself as capable ... but that is all. You are not a success, yet. You are not proven, yet. But you are sure of what you want and sure of what will be expected of you, which in my opinion is something worth feeling good about.

You finished the last chapter establishing the mindset specific to you that will lead you to realizing your potential. Now you need a powerful driving force to initiate action. You need intention, and not the kind that remains only within you—it must be publicized as well. This level of intent should enforce a degree of self-accountability that honors the efforts you have made privately so far. Those who avoid following through with action are simply discussing ideas and desires, whereas you are forming yourself into a competitor driven by intentions and needs.

WELCOME TO THE WORLD

Let me be crystal clear on something right now. You may have bought this book because you thought you wanted to shock the world, but by the time I am done with you my hope is that you *feel the need* to shock the world. That you will come to feel that realizing your potential is your calling, your purpose, and a necessity within your life (more on this in chapter 8). The need to do something is a special kind of energy that can bring out the very best in us and hold us accountable to action. The intentions behind such needs are important, however, as they must be pure and come from a place of love for yourself and for what you are trying to do.

When I interviewed Benjamin Alexander for the podcast, I got to learn the story of a man who left an established career as a DJ (think concerts with tens of thousands of party-goers) to pursue his goal of becoming Jamaica's first Olympic downhill alpine skier. This was no ordinary goal. Benjamin discovered the sport of skiing soon after he turned 30, until then he had never set foot on slopes of any kind. What started as a surprisingly fun time with friends became an individual pursuit of man versus time. Benjamin examined what the process of making a Winter Olympics looked like and determined the commitment required, and in doing so, he was getting to know and understand the world he planned to shock by qualifying for the Games.

Knowing he was going to make this enormous and life-altering commitment, his first act was to announce to the DJ world he was retiring from the industry, and state his reasons why. Talk about sending a shock to your approach to life! Benji's public announcement of his intentions showed how bought in he was to the goal. By announcing it publicly an immediate action step is taken towards the end goal, with accountability established to make you follow through and do what you plan to do.

In Benjamin's case, his initial assessment revolved around whether he had the resources and support required to take up skiing for a living for the next five years—a specific, smart, and realistic step in this decision to *shock the world* of skiing and sports. It was not a rash decision; in Benjamin's mind it was something he had a need to do. One aspect of getting to this point when you are ready to *shock your approach* is that it will appear to some (and in Benjamin's case many) that you are taking a risk or behaving out of the norm. Furthermore, there may even be some who say you should reconsider you decision, that it is an act of recklessness, and who question whether you have thought it through. Well, based on our work so far: have you thought it through?

Realization Exercise

Anticipate how your initial actions will be received.

⇨ How do I expect people to respond?

⇨ Which people will most likely try to convince me not to act?

⇨ Why do I know this is the right thing for me to be doing?

MAKING THE COMMITMENT

To *shock the approach* is to take the first public step toward your ultimate goal(s). While there might be people in your life questioning your decision, it is your responsibility to convince them (and yourself) why you must do this. For every strange look you receive when you explain your intentions, reflect on the work you have done on you and your mindset up to this point. Self-reflection is vital during these moments. Your relationship with yourself can offer enormous support during the initial approach to maintain the sense of calm and collectedness required to avoid getting discouraged. As you begin your initial approach, there is a good chance you are shocking a few people. You are getting your first taste of the magnitude of the task and journey at hand, while relishing the opportunity to one day *shock the world*. (If you were wondering, Benjamin managed to shock the world of skiing in January 2022 when he qualified for the 2022 Beijing Winter Olympics).

In the next chapter, we will learn the importance community and relationships have in facilitating this journey you are opting to go on. Just understand for now that the journey has begun and you have done the foundational work to be ready. It is one thing to anticipate how your approach will be received, but how you illustrate your seriousness about your intentions will be the catalyst for the support you eventually desire.

The Approach to Action

Step One – *Discuss it with others*

Those that are either closest to you or that are part of the world that you plan to shock. Emphasize your intentions, explain the approach you will take, and deliver a crystal-clear message of why you are capable (because you are crystal clear yourself at this point).

Step Two – *Announce a decision*

If you feel that what you are taking on requires a big decision to shift your focus and possibly discontinue other ventures, then announcing the action you're taking will deliver a shock! Social media is a natural way to do this today and gives you a motivation to provide updates in the future for how you are progressing.

Step Three – *Invest in equipment, education, or experience*

Anyone can say they plan to do something but once you invest in some equipment, some necessary education (certifications or licenses), or an experience (networking event, workplace experience), you are investing in your intentions. You have to invest enough for it to feel like a commitment or big step, which is why I love the education step. Reading a "how to" book is not a true commitment, but enrolling in a class to enhance your credentials is.

Step Four – *Commit to a deadline for the initial approach*

Determine a date in the not-too-distant future when you will have dedicated enough of your time and resources to know you can realistically assess your initial commitment. You want to be able to qualify that this is something you were right to commit to; but if you don't establish some initial milestones and thresholds to meet, it is hard to assess your progress.

The greatest part of this four-step approach is the way in which it will test the quality of work you have conducted on yourself and your mindset. People will respond with questions. Social media followers might reach out and ask you to elaborate. You will be making personal and financial investments for the first time. You will be consistently challenged on how serious you are about all of this. Again, nothing we are doing here is reckless as we have done the background work, but we must remain curious during this initial approach: curious to learn what our initial support system might look like, curious to discover if there is anything we overlooked about ourselves up to this point, curious to seek information that will facilitate our personal and professional growth towards our goal.

Curiosity is a competitive state of mind born out of ambition as it gives us purpose in how we receive information. For every potentially negative response you encounter in the discussions ahead, you can be curious to learn what this individual does not understand. You are seeking information and allowing yourself to accept there will be resistance that comes in different forms throughout this journey, but you welcome it! You accept it could be information worth inheriting or a question you have a concrete response to. A curious mind will always come from a hungry person, so if you are hungry enough to *shock the world,* don't be intimidated by the feedback you encounter. Relish it. Process it. And utilize it in ways you feel is necessary.

A Declaration to Do It

This willingness to consider and commit to the approach helped Brooks Curry and I over our two-year journey towards his qualifying for the US Olympic team. When Brooks arrived on campus at LSU, nothing about his makeup was close to that of an Olympian. He did not understand what would be required of him to achieve such a feat. He had never held himself accountable for pursuing the standards required to be this competitive. He needed to mature, educate himself, and implement the necessary personal steps before talking to others about his plans to shock the world.

Privately, he and I spoke regularly about his quality of work and the progress he was making in his development. In time, he began to talk with teammates or with other coaches about what he wanted to accomplish. Then, six months into our working relationship, we were approaching the 2020 Southeastern Conference (SEC) Championships with some initial competitive pieces falling into place. Conversations began to include challenging for SEC championships as this would represent a practical and intentional action towards eventually challenging for an Olympic berth.

Embracing the standards associated with competing for a gold in arguably the most competitive conference championship meet in US college swimming is a big test of self and mindset. With the end goal being to qualify for the US Olympic team in the 100-meter freestyle relay, the act of winning the NCAA format of that very event at this level would be a loud declaration of intent towards that goal. And, that is exactly what Brooks did. SEC Champion, 100-Yard Freestyle, 2020. The first act and initial shock had happened, one big enough to draw attention, declare his intent, and make him a competitor at the NCAA level. Those initial discussions of being an elite competitor allowed for more realistic and intentional discussion on a public level of becoming a US Olympian.

That initial approach and action not only declared Brooks' intention to become a US Olympian, it confirmed that he was capable of making things happen no matter the circumstances. Those SEC Championships were in February 2020, and as we all know, COVID-19 brought the world to a halt in March 2020 and caused the rescheduling of the 2020 Olympic Games. Those months of isolation and very limited availability for practice could have been the cause of Brooks' potential and story never seeing the light of day. But leaning on the experience of his initial approach and elite performances saw him through these trying times and gave him the belief that his dream could still happen.

There Is No Time to Waste

While setbacks and adversities are always possible, you must build a belief in your destiny and your approach that is strong enough to keep anything from derailing you. No matter the opinions or preferences of others, we commit strongly to doing something because we feel it is our calling. But, in the case of Alison Hadden, she did something because time was against her.

There are so many people we get to meet in this life; and then there are a few that we are *destined* to meet. Alison Hadden was that for me. Alison reached out to me during my "women changing the world" series to tell me how the current theme of the show made her an ideal guest. Alison's career was in marketing, but she had recently come off a long battle with cancer, and during that time, started speaking publicly to share her message to "live like there is no time to waste." Alison started her own podcast "No Time to Waste" soon after being on my show, on which she interviewed cancer survivors, others affected by it, people affected by death, and motivational experts. Her guests would shed light on experiences and concepts that could help others going through tough times. After we recorded, Alison shared the news that despite recently going into remission, cancer had shown its ugly head again, and this time it was a terminal diagnosis. She was understandably emotional, she was understandably scared—but, by God, she was not beaten.

I had two virtual conversations with Alison, that's it; but I honestly think about her at some point during almost every week. She decided to take her situation and *shock the world* of cancer by discussing it, a lot! She hosted a wide range of guests on the podcast, including major household names such as Lance Armstrong, Katie Couric, and Matthew McConaughey, who saw and felt the impact her intentions were making. Despite being handed an excuse to stop and to give in to a situation life had thrown at her, she instead looked within. She looked at the woman she was, and the fiercely competitive mindset she had at her disposal, and she opted to spend the remaining days and years of her life making the greatest impact possible. She knew her value and recognized her potential, and she refused to let this ugly disease take away the opportunity she still had to *shock the world.*

On January 29th, 2022 Alison passed away, having competed against cancer and giving it all it could handle. She left behind a standard for how humans can approach adversity and hardship, and I will feel her impact on me for the rest of my time here on earth. If there is any episode of the podcast you decide to go and check out, make it episode 52 and listen to Alison's message.

While Alison had no option but to act *when* she did, the *way* she reacted was not simply a result of the situation. It was a product of her truest self, the Alison she had invested time in and worked on throughout life, and it represented the mindset she had shown up with for years. You have been armed with the tools to invest in and work on you; the question left to answer now is: what situation must life throw at you in order for you to take a shot?

DEDICATE TO YOURSELF NOW MORE THAN EVER

Benjamin's intentions were clear. Alison's intentions were clear. Their decisions to initiate their approach towards shocking the world were something they simply needed to do in order to honor their optimal selves. The work you've done so far was born out of an idea and belief that you have the potential to shock the world. Having started the process, the work you have done so far should confirm this is something you want even more. You should know whether this is something you must do to honor your optimal self, or something you would rather remain an idea.

As you consider this first action step, how will you best utilize this version of yourself you are learning to love? What impact is this true version of yourself capable of making? How do you feel when considering the magnitude of your initial actions? As your body and mind speak louder to you, listen to them, honor them. Allow them to define the intensity behind your intention.

Realization Exercise

Create three statements of intent towards your initial approach about the following:

The Present

- Effective today, I plan to...

    e.g., start pursuing my MBA

The People in your life

- I will tell...

    e.g., my family I am going back to school

The Overall Goal (the shock)

- This is going to help me achieve the ultimate goal of...

    e.g., realizing my potential of becoming the CEO of a non-profit I plan to start

---

You have appointed yourself as the CEO of your intention and mission to shock the world. You have opted to take an initial step towards realizing your potential that notifies those closest to you of your overall objective. This calling you have will live at your core and shine outward as energy that people see and are drawn to. It will become synonymous with how people see and think of you. While it will intimidate some, it will inspire others. While it will isolate you at times, it will then connect you to others. It is essential, therefore, to insert yourself into communities capable of facilitating your intentions with reliable relationships. With the foundational phase complete, it is time to challenge ourselves, our process, and our actions further.

You are ready to Shock the Approach because

⇨ You know how you plan to invest yourself and resources into your initial step.

⇨ You have anticipated how your approach will be received by those closest to you.

⇨ You have a clear initial intention to announce your approach publicly.

Why we should Shock the Approach

| Make a Decision | Make an Announcement | Make a Commitment | Make it Happen |

SHOCK
THE COMMUNITY

INWARD STEP

How are you feeling at this point? Hopefully you are detecting some momentum and a sense of purpose. With a foundational focus on yourself, your mindset, and your initial approach in place, you must now know who is in this with you. Who will influence you? Who will tell you what you need to hear? Who will pick you up? Who can you trust? Welcome to the world away from the world you plan to shock. Think of this as your village, whether the people within it are near or far (we can have a virtual village; it's 2022 after all), they believe in you, are available to you, influence you, and are a part of you. But, for this to be a community, there must be a particular characteristic that those within it have in common. In the case of this community, that common characteristic is *you*.

People are brought together in your community (as opposed to simply ending up together) because of common intentions and shared ideals and, in some cases, to support a cause. Every political campaign is a creation of a community. Every reality TV show like "The X Factor" and "American Idol" requires the creation of a community for those competing. Again, in these examples, a community will support and facilitate the chance for a person to go shock the world of politics or the music industry. This community they have created, however, is not the world they are targeting. It is an isolated launchpad allowing for the end goal to be realized.

THE ROLE OF RELATIONSHIPS

Before you can have the ideal community, you need to create it, starting by ensuring you don't sacrifice any of your great work up to this point in order to establish it. Your sense of self, mindset, and approach must be accepted within this community. This does not mean these things can never be challenged; but if they are attacked, disrespected, or deemed inadequate, you need to act accordingly, which brings me to the glue that allows for a community to flourish.

Relationships

When approached correctly, being in a relationship with someone is a privilege. For it to be recognized as a relationship it must be honored and treated as such by both parties involved.

Realization Exercise

List five individuals outside of your family that you consider yourself to have a relationship with based on these principles:

1. I feel they bring to the relationship what I bring to it.

2. I feel they want what is best for me the same way I do.

3. I feel they tell me what I need to hear when I need to hear it.

If you're one of the fortunate ones, then you were able to come up with five names here. But the disappointing reality for most people is that this is a difficult, if not impossible, exercise. Between Facebook friends, Instagram followers, coworkers, and LinkedIn connections, you might have a population in the thousands of people you know, or to whom you are connected. But with what percentage of these people have you actually built relationships? Being the optimist that I am, I'm going to assume everyone was able to name at least three (if you could not confidently name one that's fine; that is why you are here, and I will get to you).

For those people you listed, can you identify common threads that connect them? Whether it is personality type, career background, experiences, education, achievements, or something else, try to find a couple of commonalities, as this will be the beginning of your community. For example, when I started my coaching and consulting practice, I created a community (unbeknownst to those in it) that would allow me to shape the following identity, principles, and characteristics within it:

- **Proven results in their respective industry surpassing 20 years**

- **Great listeners with good hearts**

- **Awareness and first-hand experience of other coaching and consulting firms**

- **Comfortable enough with me to tell me "No!" or when I should stop**

- **Honest enough to admit when they don't have answers**

Despite not knowing they were part of a growing community, they all recognized my potential, my desire, and my vision, and they didn't even blink before offering to be of service to me. I already knew these people, and they were relationships that had already been built. While anticipating their willingness to support me in starting and building a business, it was not with any assumption of them "doing me a favor" or something I would take for granted. This was very much a relationship-led approach to building a community, but it can also be created from scratch (I told you I'd come back to you folks that could not put a name on that list from earlier).

Transform As One

Rue Mapp is the founder and CEO of Outdoor Afro, a not-for-profit organization that celebrates and inspires connections and leadership within nature amongst the Black community. The goal is to encourage members of the black community to get into nature so as to reap the benefits that come from being outdoors, such as improved health, wider networks, and a stronger societal presence. Today, they have more than 60,000 people actively involved within their network and are the national leader in the United States for bringing Black people and nature together.

I had the luxury of learning from Rue when I had her on the podcast during the height of the pandemic and the racial disruption across the United States following George Floyd's killing in the summer of 2020. During a time of uproar and disarray across the country, Rue seemed like an ideal guest to come join me and share her experiences and examples of what it takes to bring people together. Rue shared her story of founding a community-based company in spite of perceived and actual differences both within and outside of the Black community.

Amongst the many perspectives Rue introduced to me, her story convinced me that any community can be created within this world as long as the intentions behind it are pure and clearly understood. Rue also spoke of the importance of ensuring that you "have people in the same lane that you are." This is why the value of shocking yourself, your mindset, and your approach are crucial first steps before shocking the community that you either insert yourself into or build around you. The last thing you would ever want is to be responsible for a community and then realize you are uncertain or uneducated about what you need or want from them.

At the heart of Outdoor Afro is a mission of transformation, so much so that Rue considers this the very business they are in: "the business of transformation." While this is a key component of their business model and identity, it is an integral part of what makes their community what it is. Outdoor Afro creates communities of transformation. Black people have been made aware of accessible resources to help get in touch with themselves, while surrounded by others doing the same, and while immersed in nature. Rue's community model which started as a blog from her kitchen table has transcended itself into a movement.

Through Rue's mission, the organization's 90 volunteer leaders, and thousands upon thousands of members, the Outdoor Afro community is changing who represents those getting out and leading in the outdoors. Community has been at the center of their business of transformation. As the community has grown and strengthened, Rue's mission has strengthened, illustrating the potential power a community can offer one person's mission.

What if you were at the heart of a community that encouraged and represented transformation? Is that not what we should want from any community we are a part of, never mind one we are responsible for? To go from the hope to the knowledge that you will shock the world, you must take ownership of the impact and the availability you expect from your community. Those involved in your community must be driven to facilitate the transformation of you as your journey enters the unknown.

Realization Exercise

Build it and they will come.

⇨ List 3 expectations for how your community will help realize your potential.

⇨ List 5 personal qualities community members must therefore have.

⇨ List 3 expectations you have for yourself to honor your community.

COMMUNITY FROM SCRATCH

Whether you feel great about your existing relationships within your network or if you feel like you are starting solo, you have the means to make your community what it needs to be. I've said it before and will likely say it again: the work you have done up to this point will serve you well now. When you identified what you love and are learning to love about yourself, you identified potential components of the community. When shaping the mindset you would require from analyzing established success stories, you were identifying potential characteristics of the community. The more you embrace that you know you best, the more you should know what you need around you. If you rushed through the previous exercise or were frustrated with your answers, go back and patiently consider the answers you have inside of you.

Remember earlier when I mentioned the privilege of being in a relationship with someone? I really meant that. My clients who have struggled to be heard, or who have sensed people don't value their time as much as they should, have learned how to incorporate this philosophy. It requires valuing yourself enough to know that people must view your time and energy as worthwhile and not take it for granted. That's why you are in relationships. It's a commitment of how you intend to show up for one another. And, if you are choosing to build your community from scratch, then you can be excited to know that, when done the right way, it will produce relationships such as these. You are shaping and constructing a community for yourself built upon the very principles I just outlined here in a relationship.

- You are shaping a community people want to be in.

- You are establishing value and respect for how people will be treated.

- You are emphasizing the commitment you are expecting from all involved.

- You are demonstrating, through action, the privilege it is to be a part of this community.

The final part of this that cannot be overlooked is how you will hold yourself accountable to these principles above everything. And you must! No community stands a chance if the common bond that all members share (remember that you are the common bond) is not taking their responsibilities seriously. Community members will see right through you if you are not valuing self-accountability. Consider, for instance, how it will be received by a community member if you expect them to be available for advice on short notice, but they learn you have no sense of immediacy in applying their advice. If you lead someone in your community to perceive you need their insight urgently, you better back that up by applying the insight immediatcly.

Furthermore, the standards you set will be the measuring stick for what you allow and don't allow within your community. This does not need to be a formal hiring and firing system because, like me, people may not even know they are in a community. But when you sense someone is not making the impact you were hoping for or matching the purpose you have for what you are trying to accomplish, just move on. As long as you addressed the principles you were looking for in a community member and are embodying them yourself, you can prioritize those who respect what you are trying to accomplish.

Your goals are too great to not set the tone for what you need from your community. Respect that. Enforce that. Never allow for it to be compromised. No matter how short or long a period you need this community around for, their accountability to you and your cause will be influenced directly by your ability to lead by example. Force them to take you seriously and be motivated to support you by the example you set for what you plan to accomplish.

Build It and They Will Come

Not all communities need to be a lifetime commitment or even an all-day every day experience. If you have clearly articulated and established what the community is serving you for, then you should be able to identify the parameters it exists within. Back in April 2021, I created a 27-day community, and, had I not done so, this particular book probably would not have been written. People don't achieve unique and life-changing results alone. So, when I knew Brooks Curry had a chance to make the 2020 Olympic Games in Tokyo, and I was satisfied with the 12-week training plan I felt was required to get him there, I went to the rest of the swimmers at LSU. The thing was, within this training plan was a phase of training I felt was required to convince Brooks he would be ready. One that, were he able to get through it successfully, he would feel bullet-proof for it. But I knew it was too much to ask him to do it alone.

So, in the words of Jerry Maguire, I turned to the team and asked "who's coming with me?" Not to the Olympics, and in most cases not even to the Olympic trials. No, I needed people to sacrifice their energy and their downright toughness, during what was an optimal training time in the season, to take on a 27-day training block in the middle of my plan where we would not take a day off from training.

To achieve greatness, you must be a product of greatness. That means working with great people, building great relationships, making great sacrifice, and a having a great community. Brooks was never going to become an Olympian by doing it alone. Sure, I could create a bulletproof blueprint for what he needed to do physically, but I could not be the voice and energy of an entire training group, and neither could he. After appealing to an initial group of around 35 swimmers, and stating my reasons why it would be in one of their teammate's and the program's best interest to join forces for 27 days straight, 13 athletes decided they were up for the challenge. The "why" behind this community was built on two key elements:

- We would work, hurt, sacrifice, celebrate, support, and respect all 15 members of the community (13 athletes and 2 coaches).

- We all had the opportunity to benefit from this experience; as athletes, as people, and as teammates.

The awkward part of this whole idea, however, was how it was born out of surrounding just one person with the environment they needed. It sounds selfish on the surface, right? But if you stop and think about it, who do you think held the greatest responsibility to show up and embody the two foundations of this 27-day community that I just outlined? All eyes were on Brooks within this training phase. He was the reason for our doing this, so he had to show up as a great athlete, person, and teammate every day. But having created this community, my own accountability was obviously an essential part of this as well. Fortunately, there are few things in this world that excite me more than empowering, challenging, supporting, and celebrating a group with a shared vision and collective spirit to realize potential. The feedback from all participants was unanimous.

- *The hardest phase of training in my life*

- *Never felt the need to complain one time*

- *Total trust in the process*

- *So glad I chose to be involved*

There it is: hard work, positive mindset, trust, appreciation for being involved. If you're not sure where to start in terms of what you need to prioritize from your community, reflect on ways to incorporate:

- A hard-working approach

- A consistently positive outlook

- Trust in yourself and one another

- A sense of the privilege of being involved

Because, if you can shape a community built of people like this, just think about what that will do for you, your relationships, and your journey. It won't just be you smashing through that glass pane, it will be a collective effort.

COMPETITIVE COLLABORATION

If you are someone working in a performance-based industry, I have to share one of my favorite terms here for something that I became aware of long before I named it. "Competitiveness" and "collaboration" as individual terms are typically welcomed and sought after across a variety of fields today, particularly those that come with performance expectations. Each word, however, has its limitations on its own. Competitiveness gets you so far when you tackle things alone, but what happens when your success plateaus and even dries up? Who is there to push and support you then? Collaboration is great when a group of unique and diverse perspectives come together, but is everyone honestly bringing their everything to the collaboration? Is someone doing most of the work and others going along for the ride?

"Competitive collaboration" is a professional relationship where all parties involved enter into it with the understanding that they will get out of it what they are willing to put in to it. Those within a partnership or a community are curious about how they can best serve the competitive collaboration. They are eager to grow through the process and are driven by an accountability of themselves and of each other. Competitive collaboration, ladies and gentlemen, is where the beauty of a community can start to take on an optimal level of purpose. It is a momentum that simply cannot be stopped. You recognize the efforts and results you wish to see from others will be a direct return on the investment that you are willing to make in the select few around you. So, if competitive collaboration is the goal, how do you approach the shaping of this community to ensure that you eventually attain it?

THIS IS NO ONE-TIME THING

One of my favorite parts of my podcast is that I meet entrepreneurs who are sometimes just getting started or just becoming known for what they do. Then I get to sit there and listen to all the reasons why—based primarily on who they are, and also on their ideas—they are going to be a major success. Darrien Mikel shocked the world of recruitment and hiring through his business Qualifi, which is an on-demand phone interview platform capable of making the hiring process seven times faster. Within the first two years of the company's history, Darrian was already winning local awards as a leader and entrepreneur, while similarly the company was being recognized as one of the great places to work.

When I interviewed Darrien, it took very little time to build a rapport with him based on our shared love of competing, sports, and realizing potential. As you can imagine, Darien loved everything about the idea of Qualifi and what it had to offer, but he did not know how to realize it's true potential by himself. Along with his brother Devin, Darrien chose to seek out collaboration in order to build a community he felt was required to build a trusted foundation for the company to thrive over time. Whenever Darien was unsure, he looked to collaborate. When he didn't have the experience, he looked to collaborate. He was building collaborative relationships with people who wanted to see him succeed. Furthermore, he was establishing the very ideals that the company could rely upon as it grew. Collaborate first to achieve the best result. Lean on the established communities, especially as success and growth become factors. Look inward and ask, "Are we still collaborating? Are we still trusting the community?"

> **Realization Exercise**
>
> Reach out to a member of your community and collaboratively work towards your potential.
>
> ⇨ Request direction on how to incorporate advice and then look for ways to assess.
>
> ⇨ Have them challenge your knowledge of your process and create ideas for overcoming issues.
>
> ⇨ Demand honesty in feedback and then create a system for accountability.

There is no denying that there is a widely diverse list of characteristics and principles that can help realize potential. But a deliberately created community is an optimal path to fulfilling your potential. Like Qualifi, the idea and vision must be solid; but an isolated idea is a limited idea from the very beginning. Darrian's collaborative mind, advocacy for community, and willingness to build a competitive foundation makes his community airtight.

Embrace Everything That Comes with It

The competitive element of competitive collaboration comes through in how seriously we prioritize the role of our community. A competitor will see their community as a launchpad for the processes and actions required for handling each stage of their development. The wins will be felt and the achievements will be celebrated, but the intentions of the community will always ensure that the progress continues.

By accepting the direct impact community can have on your future growth and performance, you suddenly want to embrace the need to build it now. A community of specific ideals, with a common commitment towards facilitating your potential, is waiting for you to act, to initiate the building of relationships, and to demonstrate how it is a privilege to be a part of it. They relish the notion of being involved in a collaborative culture that is curious about consistently growing while striving to compete at higher levels. People are naturally drawn to healthy change and success, and you are specifically trying to implement both into your journey.

Invite others along for the ride. Make sure you know why you need them. Take the time to address the role you see them playing, and embrace being the common characteristic that brings certain people together. After all, they are only involved because they see in you what you see: the ability to *shock the world.*

You are ready to Shock the Community because

⇨ You understand the people you need within it to facilitate your growth.

⇨ You realize you will need to put into relationships what you seek to get out of them.

⇨ You know the roles and responsibilities of all community members, especially yourself.

Why we should Shock the Community

| Build Expectations | Build Relationships | Build Accountability | Build Growth |

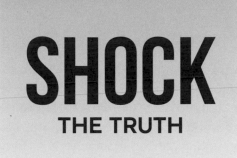

SHOCK
THE TRUTH

When you have coached a decade around college athletes you learn ways to effectively problem solve. The athletes I worked with would provide accounts of events or issues they were experiencing and, as the coach, I would listen to what they had to say. While I listened to an individual share with me their version of the truth, I would always ask myself, "What is happening here?" Not in the actual moment while I was listening to them, but in the larger sense of what was behind this conversation. How did we get to this point? What is not being said, seen, or accepted by this athlete that they have yet to consider or mention? Usually, the answer to the last question falls under the category of **the truth**.

It is normal as you encounter perceived problems in the midst of a process with a lot at stake to simply respond in the moment. Pertaining to your process to *shock the world* we will refer to adversity and potential roadblocks as a *truth*, in the sense that a truth is being revealed, accepted, and owned. This is a level of ownership within your journey that will keep you from taking things personally, becoming deflated, or even wanting to just quit. When you and your community consider challenging scenarios as truths, the hope is to respond with a heightened desire to combat whatever you are encountering. Whether that is with internal analysis or through discussion, it will shape your approach and your processes moving forward. You will start to create a contingency plan to help respond to such truths in the future.

You Cannot Accept What You Don't Identify

I have met a number of people over the years that have demonstrated what a life of embracing the truth looks like, but few have embraced it in the way that Lex Gillette has. A two-time Paralympic silver medalist in the long jump and world record holder in the event, Lex has been blind since midway through childhood. Balancing the demands of being a professional athlete and motivational speaker, Lex's story was one of those I simply needed to hear for myself.

Before we spoke, I knew he was a champion and a highly committed athlete, but I was eager to learn how he was able to strive to such heights despite the challenging lifestyle that comes with being blind. Lex's success was born out of the closest community to him—his family, specifically his mother. When Lex's sight became an issue at eight years old, his mother had two choices: resist what was happening or embrace the truth that her son would lose his sight.

Over those next few years, his mother's choice to love and guide her son based on the reality of his situation provided Lex the foundation to optimize his God-given talent as an athlete. A mother saw what her son needed and armed him with the necessary tools to live his life as a competitor. His go-to saying of "there's no need for sight when you have a vision" exemplifies how he accepts his greatest truth in life and the willpower it has provided him to optimize life.

While it was the acceptance of a *physical* limitation that Lex had to deal with, the catalyst for his success was his mother's choice to highlight and accept the truths in her son's life. At eight years old, Lex's mom was still very much in the driver's seat. She chose to look another eight years down the road and took control of the process ahead accordingly. She became the strength that Lex needed by lifting him up emotionally. She then shifted gears by addressing and teaching the life skills Lex would need in order to navigate the real world, blind. Simply put, she taught her son that he "gets to decide what he does and no one else." As a result, Lex was then able to implement the same approach to future struggles in his journey, which is what makes the story so relevant from a process perspective. What are you willing to accept as truth, and what are you willing to do about it?

Realization Exercise

List major truths you have experienced, but were not responsible for, within a recent process.

⇨ How were truths accepted and embraced?

⇨ How were truths dismissed and even ignored?

⇨ What kind of outcomes resulted from either way these were handled?

What eventually has to be accepted is that the truth can only be hidden and tamed for so long. At some point, it will come out and make the impact it wants to. And as you start the process of pursuing and revealing truths, the biggest truth of all starts to play its greatest role.

The truth scares people!

Don't you think embracing and accepting a life of being blind wasn't scary for an eight-year-old Lex? Don't you think I empathize with you as you're looking at the list you just made identifying significant truths you faced that were or weren't embraced? And don't you think it was scary for me, for Brooks, and for the other athletes to learn I might not have a job next season, three weeks out from Olympic trials?

ADDRESS WHAT YOU ARE EXPERIENCING

It was the only thing I had not planned for, and frankly had no reason for it to be on my radar. Specifically, LSU men had just had the highest national finish in 20 years. They had exciting recruits already lined up for the next two recruiting classes, and all signs pointed to being in a good position to make history with their first-ever US Olympian. But the administration felt it was time for change, and they mutually agreed to part ways with my then-boss and friend of almost 10 years, Dave Geyer, three days before our contracts would have to be renewed for another season.

When you are a member of staff under the head coach, even second-in-command like I was, nothing is guaranteed. Despite having the choice to just quit and still get paid for three more months, I was not about to leave the athletes I had poured my heart and soul into (and who had done exactly the same to me and more). I was offered the chance to coach athletes to Olympic trials despite no reassurance of a job upon my return. But in the moment, on that day I found out and the 24 hours after, I was a broken man.

When your team and sport received minimal support as ours did by an administration, creating the environment required to send athletes to the Olympics, never mind to do so representing the United States, takes a lot of work. Between the efforts of people like myself, head coach Dave, and the athletes themselves, we had to create an elite culture from within. So, you can imagine how, when it's ripped away from you in an instant without warning, it can cut really deep. The first truth I had to accept was even though this was happening to me, this wasn't about me. This was about the athletes. This was about finishing what had been started. Specifically, there was a common consensus within the team that we could still make history as a program. No matter how I felt, my personal situation could not be why this could no longer happen. That is why, the day after the news, I addressed the guys going to the Olympic trials and made the next and most important truth as clear as I could.

Speaking through tears and raw emotion I simply stated, "I cannot promise that I will be able to show up as the best version of myself the next three weeks, but you have to promise yourselves and me that you will show up as the best version of you … because this isn't about me, this is all about you." It's impossible to know how the story of Shock the World would have ended had my job not been on the line. But what I do know is that by acknowledging the fullest extent of the truth, the preparation to perform at optimal levels was undisturbed and, possibly, even enhanced.

Realization Exercise

Identify at least one truth in your daily process that can free you of an issue by considering

⇨ The ways you speak to yourself or how you treat those around you

⇨ The ways you pursue improvements or handle adversities

⇨ The ways you use your time, prioritize tasks, or generate opportunities

How will identifying this truth improve your process moving forwards?

THE REALITY OF THE TRUTH

When you started this book, I asked you to be open and honest with yourself about what you love and don't love about yourself, which required the revealing of some private truths. The difference here is that none of this part is private. And this is no longer just about you. You are in the process and you have a community invested in this process with you. Now is not the time to be prideful and show a reluctance to learn the truth. As the old saying goes, "The truth will set you free." By incorporating that same sentiment into our process, think of how freeing things can become when you search for, examine, and embrace truths along the way. Searching for truths can become an empowering process as roadblocks become mere speed bumps, and the road ahead will be one that you welcome.

Truths will guide the process. When we address truths, they guide us to where we want to go; otherwise, we create paths to avoid them, steering ourselves away from our goal. Often the truth is reframed as a belief or a perspective, allowing room for negotiation about why or how something is. When working with clients in the sales industry I encounter this a lot. Frustration builds when leads are not converted into clients, and the salespeople formulate their own perspective on why it didn't work out. So, much like when I worked with athletes, I initiate a discussion to reveal "what is happening here." I pursue it as finding the path most likely to reveal a truth as opposed to a perspective or a belief. Are you consistently struggling to close deals? Identify a truth in the pitch, the delivery, or telling signs in the client. The beauty of truth is that despite being difficult to find sometimes and scary to face, when embraced it can remove a lot of time wasted elsewhere.

While I reference how I coach people to reveal truths, it is important to note this is not a greenlight to simply tell others their truths. I wholeheartedly believe that a person's process is 100 times more likely to be impacted when a truth is sought after and discovered as opposed to shoved in their face. As a coach, my job is to facilitate the personal discovery of truths within someone's process, especially at first. Some of my clients have developed the capacity to seek out the truth, so much so that we can have professional business discussions about a truth of theirs worth discussing (did someone say competitive collaboration?). But this is an important principle to accept especially for leaders. Demonstrate through your processes how you embrace truths and mentor others on how to do the same. Before long everyone will be looking at processes, target audiences, goals, and much, much more with a heightened awareness in the pursuit of truths and eventually optimal success.

It Is Okay to Go in Search of It

To shock the world, sometimes you must, firstly, have the ability to either see truths or accept truths that others don't see or accept, before secondly, doing something about it. Jesse Cole, owner of the Savannah Bananas, joined my podcast back in 2020 (again, right before he and they really became the household names or TikTok celebrities that they very much are today). The mission of the Savannah Bananas is "Fans First, Entertain Always" and since 2016, they have been reinventing how Baseball is presented to the paying audience. There is nothing they do as an organization without asking the question, "Is this fans first?" which, as Jesse mentioned, has provided a sense of vision to those working in the organization when it comes to their role—they are themselves fans first, before they are employees.

Having grown up playing and being around the sport of baseball most of his adult life, Jesse Cole felt there were opportunities beyond the very narrow and outdated boundaries that baseball offered from an entertainment standpoint. He believed in the truth that baseball had the ability to entertain, and he was hell-bent on showing the world his truth. Why not have impromptu dance parties that are initiated by the players? Why not have the announcer come to home plate and take a pitch in the middle of the game? Why not have drones flying around the field broadcasting the game online? These few examples of what The Savannah Bananas followed through with and did during games embody Jesse's mission of "fans first" entertainment. It is a mission that flips the very spectacle of a baseball game on its head by making the game as much about the fans as it is about the game itself.

Jessie went in search of more truths by firstly making new and revolutionary ways to entertain fans a part of his process, and then by watching the fans experience the entertainment live. For as much data as you can try to collect through questionnaires and taking polls, nothing tells the truth about an experience more than simply watching it unfold. Jesse strived to reveal as many truths as possible about the fan experience because that was how he intended to shock the world of not just baseball, but the entertainment industry too.

When an idea of theirs didn't work, a truth was revealed. When an idea hit, a truth was revealed. Jesse's market research was guiding his process of making the Savannah Bananas "the greatest show in sports." The community that Jesse built inside the organization was built on the premise that no idea was a bad idea and that creativity was essential, along with risk-taking. As the leader, Jesse has very much walked this walk in every sense: he has supported and channeled the sharing of ideas; he has taken ownership of the possibility they might not work; he has even stood up in front of a sellout crowd wearing a banana-colored tuxedo to be the face of every part of the show, good or bad (he wore the same suit to our interview).

Jesse Cole and the Savannah Bananas are a result of many incredible strokes of marketing, business, and entrepreneurial genius. But their willingness to reveal and embrace truths in their process is something to admire alongside anything they've achieved. They are curious about what can be discovered by examining and revealing what is happening. They are flexible and open-minded enough to accept realities that invoke change and growth towards reaching their full potential. As an organization, they wear their identity, community, and truths on their sleeve for the world to see and have an incredible amount of fun in the process.

As I mentioned earlier, by embracing truths we can streamline our process greatly and avoid wasting time on discussions and processes that do not embrace what is really happening. Nothing about this part of the process is easy, but it does get easier over time. You just have to start—and recognize the power that comes from implementing this. The truth really does set you free, and the freeing energy that builds within your process will spark the kind of action you want to move closer to realizing your potential.

You are ready to Shock the Truth because

⇨ You know that by seeking truths you are revealing ways to enhance your process.

⇨ You sense the freedom that comes with embracing truths in your process.

⇨ Every truth connects you more to both your identity and overall intentions.

Why we should Shock the Truth

> Clarity
> in Situation
>> Clarity
>> in Issue
>>> Clarity
>>> in Self
>>>> Clarity
>>>> in Process

SHOCK
THE HABITS

The first and final 30 minutes of my day play an essential part in what I get out of the many hours between them. When I was coaching swimming, I spent the time from 4:45 a.m. to 5:15 a.m. waking up, getting caught up with the world, and visualizing what practice would need to look like. Then I would set off for the pool and still be 15 minutes early for the workout. My days typically ended with me tying up loose ends on my phone and zoning out with the TV, not really an ideal way to promote good sleep or optimal recuperation overnight for my brain and body. I never thought it was an issue. However, since starting my own coaching practice, my first and final 30 have changed—and wow, have I felt the impact. Today my first and final 30 involves one of three things: writing, reading, or talking. If it does not stimulate my attention or my creative imagination, then it does not touch my first and final 30. Why be so strict about this? Because the habits I start and end my day with have massive potential to dictate the quality of my habits throughout the day as well.

I can proudly say I have consistently embodied a healthy and fit lifestyle. When I got to my thirties, I noticed I was getting asked more often, "Man, how do you stay looking so fit?" And I would answer, "Oh, I just never really let myself get out of shape. It's just always been a habit of mine to be fit, I guess." Then people would give me a couple of examples of what they called bad habits to explain why they had gotten out of shape (not that I would ask, but people just like to tell you why for some reason). After hearing about bad habits like excessive drinking, overindulging in fast food, and poor time management, typically I am then informed how their schedule and people in their life cause these bad habits. I would typically wish them well and let them know that if I could ever be of use to them, I'm here. Considering the chapter you just read, however, can you detect what is absent here when considering who should take full ownership for these bad habits? The truth!

THERE IS A PROBLEM HERE

The truth about so-called good and bad habits is that they are better labelled good habits and problems. This chapter is one of action, making it vital that you have the right type of habits to facilitate action. You have a strong and thriving community behind you. You have a heightened curiosity towards identifying truths in your process. Therefore, if you notice a consistent absence of certain habits required to take action, you have a problem. In my example of someone who is striving to get in shape, the diet and lifestyle they currently have is not enabling them to be fit and healthy, which means it is a problem. By labeling it a problem you admit wrongdoing on your part and take ownership that something has to be done to rectify the problem. But this is an action chapter; why am I being all negative and harping on about problems?

Realization Exercise

Identify a bad habit that can be redefined as a problem (related to realizing your potential).

⇨ What about this problem has a detrimental impact on you as a person/competitor?

⇨ What about this problem hurts your process and ability to perform?

⇨ What has prevented you from addressing this problem sooner?

What makes addressing bad habits as problems powerful is the way a slight shift in definition can be a catalyst for change. Some of life's greatest habits are born out of problems. A smoker does not stop smoking because smoking is a bad habit; they stop it and implement better habits when they address it as the life-threatening problem it is. If you want to *shock the world* then you must identify problems that have prevented you from doing so already and replace them with reliable habits. While competitors around you will be frustrated and not address their "bad habits," you will be identifying opportunities to launch yourself forward from the slingshot of your problems. The greatest athletes in their respective sports have made their names on the back of this approach, and I was fortunate to interview a sporting great back in 2020.

FOLLOW THE CODE

Shaun Tomson is one of surfing's all-time greats and is a man who has had equally impressive careers both as an athlete and as an entrepreneur. Shaun spent the first half of his life consistently shocking the world of surfing by pushing new thresholds in his sport as he integrated the habits necessary to do such things. He even invented what is a commonly used skill in surfing today known as "the thruster" and was one of the first athletes to embrace the notion of "flow state" in competition. He identified areas in his process to improve and separate himself as a competitor, then implemented the habits necessary to optimize his performance.

Despite Shaun being such a game-changer in every sense as an athlete, you can argue that his work post-surfing has been equally, if not more, impactful. Following his athletic career and the creation of two successful clothing businesses, Shaun decided to begin motivating greater intentions and purposes in others. To do this, Shaun presents *The Surfer's Code* to companies and people the world over. It involves 12 lines of "I will" statements to promote commitments to life and bring people together through building awareness of shared values. Now that is one powerful way to get someone to acknowledge a problem and completely shift their intentions towards habits to live by.

The Surfer's Code that Shaun presents stems from his belief that we are all capable of establishing the power within our lives "to be better and to help others be better." Even more powerful, by committing to such work, Shaun believes a true purpose in life can be established. Envisioning how a problem can evolve into a life purpose might seem a little far-fetched at this moment for you, but it starts with committing to the right habits. The longer that commitment lasts, the more consistency is built; and a competitor with consistent habits has the potential to *shock the world.*

Realization Exercise

Either using the same problem you identified earlier or a new one...

⇨ How can this problem launch you towards a new habit?

⇨ How can this new habit be best incorporated into your process?

⇨ How will this habit influence and establish your purpose moving forward?

Something like a code, a strong community, or even a set of truths will offer the guidelines for the types of habits that are worth embodying. This is a chapter of action after all. So how can we look towards building consistency and trust in our habits?

Growing What You Have Established

A habit isn't like riding a bike. It must be tried, tested, nourished, re-examined, challenged, improved upon ... and then we start the process over again. Athletes pick up new habits, otherwise known as skills, all the time. A golfer doesn't stop practicing the tee shot the first time they hit one down the center of the fairway. A gymnast doesn't stop learning how to perform a somersault the first time they land on their feet. That's just the moment of discovery when a habit or skill is first implemented. They understand and respect the continuous rehearsal and repetition that lies ahead, which is why athletes are such creatures of habit. The respect an athlete has towards habits directly correlates to what they can expect out of competition.

While framing bad habits as problems can launch us into pursuing beneficial habits, the implementation of the right habit can raise the expectations we have of ourselves. As we go through the cycle of implementing, developing, and building upon a habit, we get a residual reward of positive reinforcement. *The proof is in the pudding* as they say. When you sense habits are guiding your actions towards improved performance, you are not only appreciating the progress, you feel incentivized to invest more in the very habits that got you there.

This is no time to be humble, folks. If your habits are guiding you (and potentially others) down the road you want to go down, then celebrate that! Then double down on that investment. Can those habits be built upon? What other habits need to be considered? And to fuel your growing excitement, just think how much more you can grow and come to expect of yourself. Not only will your habits continue to fuel you, but they will be witnessed by those around you and fuel them too.

As the CEO of Axis Entertainment, Sarah Miller understands the value of habits for both herself and those she leads. Axis Entertainment is an award-winning experiential agency that drives leadership, influence, and authority through public relations and events. It is a company that serves its clients through consistent action and personal engagement, so you can imagine the importance of a CEO that prioritizes a similar approach in themselves. Sarah's story is one of continually raising standards for both herself and her business, which is why her clients trust her in the world of branding, marketing, and event management. By embracing the practice of setting and attaining high standards in her work (Axis has been an annual recipient of *Best in Public Relations* awards in the state of California for the past decade), her expectations for herself consistently remain at the highest levels too. She instills confidence in clients that, if they implement the right habits, they too can reap the rewards.

When habits lead you down a path to success in one part of life, they can also become your instinctual response in other areas when you need them most. Sarah revealed to me that her approach to becoming a high-profile businesswoman was the very same approach she took over a 6-year period when going through five brain surgeries for a brain tumor that repeatedly kept affecting her. She built her career on never giving up, establishing habits of resilience, fortitude, and the highest standards in her performance, so in response to the diagnosis, she asked: *What do I need to do?* An instinctual response to form habits right away.

Sarah's operating system recognized something needed to be implemented to establish the habits required that would overcome the issues associated both with her diagnosis and response to surgeries. When going through an extensive brain surgery to remove a tumor as Sarah did (the last of which was an 18-hour surgery), one can expect to gain a lot of insight on what not to do both before and after the surgery. But despite the six months following the surgery challenging Sarah to the point of almost giving up, the competitor she is knew she had the habits required to overcome and do what needed to be done.

Realization Exercise

Getting your habits to lead you towards the path you need to be on.

⇨ What do you need to do to enforce your habits at all times?

⇨ How will you enforce making this a consistent habit to optimize performance?

⇨ How will this habit impact others and serve as a positive example?

Following a successful recovery from her surgery, Sarah continues to implement and enhance the habits that make her successful and allow her to continue improving. It is vital for optimal impact that the thresholds for your habits continue to be challenged by you raising the bar for what is required of them. By not doing so, you would be resting on the very principles that got you to where you are. Similarly, as my first and final 30 have evolved now that I'm an entrepreneur, I've seen the already strongly-established habits throughout my day expand and strengthen further too. Part of my self-accountability for my first and final 30 stems from motivating my clients to challenge themselves to do the same. It is not a necessary exercise for all my clients, and the approach to best utilize it varies. But the purpose of it is consistent; optimal habits are being utilized at an optimal frequency.

Today, when a guy asks me how I stay in such good shape, my answer to them is a question: "What do the first and final 30 minutes of your day look like?" And when they look at me like I'm changing the subject I tell them, "To implement habits for health and wellness that eventually you can live your life by, start by taking ownership of the easiest 60 minutes of your day to control." Their response? "Oh, that shouldn't be too difficult." Well then, let's see it!

You are ready to Shock the Habit because

⇨ You are willing to address bad habits as problems.

⇨ You are able to turn a problem into a catalyst for a new habit.

⇨ You are capable of motivating yourself to rely upon consistent habits.

Why we should Shock the Habit

| Implement Habit | Establish Habit | Raise Expectation | Build New Habits |

SHOCK
THE RESISTANCE

Let me introduce you to something that I've become all too familiar with having competed at an international level in my sport and coached hundreds of others. This is the one thing that prevents optimal belief, stunting confidence and creating vulnerabilities in all ensuing actions. It is something that I have deemed cancerous when thinking or talking about your ability to reach your full potential. And most of the time, by the time the signs of it show up, it's already too late.

I'm talking about DOUBT.

Doubt is the result of not knowing yourself well enough, not trusting your preparation, or not trusting the community and culture you represent. It is at the heart of the resistance preventing you from fully immersing yourself in your process and actions, and it will always try its best to spoil the party. History can certainly convince you that for every success there are many more examples of failure, so it can become ingrained in you that it is more likely you will fail than succeed.

As a sports coach, I have known some of the greatest professionals, totally prepared individuals and teams, who still encountered doubt—because it is human nature. When we have momentum and can tell things are going the way we want them to go, we actually tend to resist it. "This is going so well, somethings got to give, right?" Without realizing it we are planting seeds of doubt within our consciousness, looking to qualify why it won't be the success we want it to be. Because if we qualify why it won't work, then we don't need to fully commit; if we do not fully commit, then we are likely to fail; and when the failure comes because we opted not to fully commit, we have our reason for why we didn't. Sound familiar? It is okay to see yourself in this analogy; you should, it is human nature.

LET'S GO FIND THE CHIP

Over my time as a coach, I have encouraged the conversations created by doubt and resistance by encouraging athletes and clients to join me in the resistance. Let's get in there and get acquainted with what is happening. What I've come to find over the years is when we get into the resistance, we discover a specific person or period once sparked a feeling of resentment. As time passed, this initial grievance has evolved into a contributor to our doubt that is limiting our total commitment to the process and the actions laid out. One big chip on the shoulder, if you will. It is the reason why I have always deemed such chips as an enormous positive.

In the same way knowing truths about your process can help launch you further along within it, identifying a chip on your shoulder can provide a major internal catalyst. By embracing it, not only will this chip be able to shock the resistance enough to break it, but it can motivate future behavior if you bring it along for the ride. It can provide a constant, internal reminder of where you came from, what shaped you, and why your identity is better for having it. But as you edge closer to optimal performance and realizing your potential, there is an even more powerful role this chip can play. It can remind you that you didn't come this far simply because you wanted to; you came this far because something inside of you said you needed to.

Keely Cat-Wells is the Founder and CEO of C-Talent which is an award-winning, disabled-led talent management and consultancy company, representing high-profile deaf and disabled talent. The company works to place disabled talent into roles of all kinds within the entertainment, advertising, and media industries. Keely herself has demonstrated her ability to shock the world through her dedicated work to making social, systemic, and economic change, and has been abundantly recognized for it. Not yet 30 years old, Keely has been named One Young World Entrepreneur of the Year and Forbes 30 under 30 Entertainment honoree, and has received a variety of other awards and recognitions as well.

While so much of Keely's work and mission today is about representing a highly under-represented demographic, she is representing herself too. She developed a disability in her late teenage years while pursuing a dancing career at a prestigious dance school in England. During this time, she was repeatedly dismissed and misdiagnosed despite suffering horrendous pain in her stomach. In time, however, she found the right medical experts to correctly diagnose the issue in her intestines, but the matter did not end there. Following the initial surgery that should have been routine, an allergic reaction was caused leading to eight more surgeries, and Keely found herself fighting for her life. Despite a successful surgery that resolved her 18-month ordeal, the consequence of it was the removal of her colon, receiving a permanent ileostomy, having to wear an ileostomy bag the rest of her life, and becoming disabled.

A resistance in someone will limit them from seeing their full potential, while a resistance in an industry will limit opportunities for those willing to work and realize their talent. Keely learned from her 18-month ordeal that she could handle anything life threw at her, dealing with many of her own doubts throughout that trying time. But as impressive as her personal journey of fortitude and perseverance has been, the way she has been able to shock the resistance of the talent industry is even more impressive.

Realization Exercise

Identify when doubt creeps in and creates a resistance within you.

⇨ What is that doubt telling you about both the moment and the circumstances leading to it?

⇨ Can you identify a chip-on-the-shoulder that can serve you moving forwards?

⇨ How will that chip shift your intentions towards *having a need* to fulfil your potential?

After moving to the US, Keely shared with me how it was her own negative experience of auditioning for work in Los Angeles that was the genesis for C-Talent here in the US. Being told that she could not be considered for a role because when wearing a bikini her disability was visible, prompted Keely to act. Her intention shifted from getting work for herself as an actress to representing all those who continued to be ignored, mistreated, or mislabeled because of disabilities.

WANT VERSUS NEED

There was (and remains) a massive resistance within the entertainment industry to allowing disabled talent to realize their potential, and Keely became determined to change that. She *had a need* to ensure that disabled talent would no longer have to worry about consideration for roles and opportunities they were qualified for and capable of performing great in. Her chip-on-the-shoulder, stemming from non-acceptance and mistreatment, combined with her proven ability to endure hardship built a foundational need in her life to represent others who were experiencing hardship.

You see, when the outcome means enough to us and the impact we wish to make is great enough, we determine that this is something we *need to do*. We need the challenge. We need the competition. We even need the adversities and the resistance because they remind us how badly we need to be doing what it is we are doing.

Do you see what we've done in this chapter? It was all doom and gloom at first, laced with doubt; but from doubt, we can explore and embrace the resistance within us or at times around us. From resistance, we can identify chips on shoulders and catalysts for change. And from such discoveries, we can now have a secret weapon to venture forth with, a true need to do what it is we are doing (more on this in the next chapter).

THEY DON'T COME OFTEN

A key reason for presenting resistance in the final third of the book is because the truest form of it appears when we are approaching our breakthrough. You are arriving at a point in your journey where you are on the brink of something significant, something spectacular, a potential shock felt around your world. At this juncture, however, there is possibly something at the surface or deep down preventing you from bringing it to fruition.

Arguably my favorite part of being a swim coach was discovering resistances and knowing that, between an athlete and myself, we had just stumbled upon a key that would unlock their potential. What a feeling! You just know it when you hear it, and you realize this will be that chip-on-the-shoulder that is required to break the final resistance. It is difficult to pick one specific example above others from my decade of swim coaching, but an example that I believe reveals how deep-rooted these resistances can be involved an athlete I coached back in 2016.

Sibling rivalry is a real thing. I grew up as the younger brother to a sister two years my elder, and for the first 12 years of my life my only goal was to beat her in anything. But the problem was, I simply couldn't. She was athletic, smart, and frankly as tough as most of the boys in our neighborhood. It bothered the hell out of me for years; but once physiology and, more specifically, puberty took over, I grew a foot taller than she, and I could now keep her at arm's length (quite literally) when competing in any sport. But for one of my female athletes back in 2016, she was the younger sister to a brother who had always been the "success story" growing up.

This shadow that this young woman felt she existed in had followed her to college, even when her brother lived in another state, and by this point had even finished his athletic career. In her eyes, no matter what she accomplished in her swimming, it could not possibly be as impressive as what her brother had done. But in the spring of 2016, she and I found ourselves discussing exactly this; and it was right there that we both realized: this pressure and expectation that was preventing her from realizing her potential had no grounds to be playing such a significant role. A resentment to a situation that had long become irrelevant was still affecting her. We were able to build the argument that her career had already matched the heights of her brother's in a lot of areas. She was so accustomed to feeling "less than" her brother that she had not even fully acknowledged her achievements and growth. This moment of recognition we had stumbled upon just happened to remove a weight she had carried her entire athletic career.

In her next competition, she swam free of her brother's shadow for the first time in her life. She competed with a purpose to write her own story and deliver on the expectations she had carried for the past four years. She had gone to another level. She had shocked the resistance that had prevented her from being the nationally recognized athlete she felt she was capable of being. The result of this competition? She went one better than anything her brother had ever done and became a senior national team member. The resistance was gone forever.

Realization Exercise

Identify a long-established resistance from your past that you have never fully addressed.

⇨ How has avoiding this limited you so far in your journey towards your optimal potential?

⇨ What will it take for you to address and accept this resistance once and for all?

⇨ What would it mean for your future development to be free of this resistance?

FULFILLING THE TRUST IN YOURSELF

Whether it is through the breaking or embracing of our resistances, we are building a bulletproof trust in who we are and what we are capable of doing. When we are this sure of ourselves, we can find fulfillment—in our purpose, our process, our actions, and most importantly, in ourselves. I have had the good fortune on two separate occasions of interviewing an expert with a proven history of facilitating opportunities to help women build the belief and trust required to optimize their careers and lives.

Samantha Ettus is the founder and CEO of Park Place Payments, a best-selling author, a renowned speaker and podcast host, and was named to *Entrepreneur Magazine's* 2021 100 Women of Impact. As a trailblazer for women in business, she paves the way to create more and more opportunities for women to either find work or become their own bosses. Sam's perspective when it comes to assessing value in a day's work is an ideal place to build the trust and the fulfillment required to shape the success story we plan to be.

A question like "am I fulfilled by what I accomplished today?" prompts reflection to usher in the growth required towards trusting yourself. Consider the work Sam does with Park Place Payments as a women-owned company that offers financial services to small businesses and freelancers (most of whom are women themselves). An example we discussed on the show was that of a woman who has committed her life to being a stay-at-home mom before courageously deciding to start a small business or a side hustle.

You can understand how this would be difficult in many ways for such a woman. How would she know whether she is succeeding when first starting out? So much is new—potentially a first-time experience—while her identity may feel under threat from choosing to move away from a role she has identified with for years. That is a major resistance that needs to be shocked; otherwise, it could prevent her from sticking with it. So, when there are no past standards or experiences to assess yourself against, one place to start could be by asking: "Am I fulfilled in the work I did today?"

Realization Exercise

Consider a part of yourself that you trust completely.

⇨ What did you have to do in order to build your trust in that particular trait?

⇨ What lessons can you take from that in order to build trust in areas that are lacking it?

⇨ Are there any areas where you lack trust in yourself that could influence an existing resistance?

No individual's resistance is any more or less profound than the next person's; it is a subjective resistance pertaining to the individual's perspective. I love the idea of assessing your fulfillment in a day's work in the context of doing something entirely new and unknown. I have to think most, if not all, of you reading this are trying to do something for the first time. If you have never realized your potential, then you are doing *that* for the first time here.

If you opt to assess your fulfillment during this process, you may uncover a doubt or resistance that could reveal that you are not completely fulfilled. But we are all here for the same reason and share a similar goal, no matter how big or small the size of the task may seem. The fact is, a stay-at-home mother of 20 years choosing to start a career is shocking the world. Just because her world may seem tiny in comparison to entire industries other people assess themselves in, to them it is their *whole* world.

So, what about you? Are you fulfilled by the work you've done on yourself inwardly at this point? The work required to love yourself, build a thriving community, and be willing to insert yourself into any resistance beneath the surface is not easy. You have every reason not only to feel fulfilled at this point, but you should even be proud. And that calm and confident feeling you have that enters your body with every inhalation—that's the feeling of being ready.

You are ready to Shock the Resistance because

⇨ You are reflecting on your doubts and investigating what you can learn from them.

⇨ You are growing a trust in yourself that is constantly evolving.

⇨ You are seeking fulfillment in the work you do.

Why we should Shock the Resistance

Discover the Chip	Discover the Intentions	Discover the Need	Discover the Potential

SHOCK
THE GAP

The potential for success will be directly influenced by the process leading up to it, but it will not necessarily be guaranteed. How deflating can a realization like that feel? Not guaranteed? *You're here to tell me, Steve, that after eight chapters you can't guarantee me life-altering results and performances? That's not what this book is?* I'm afraid there are no guarantees in this book. But every client I work with, every athlete I've ever worked with, has been told the same. I have consistently stated that "my job is to ensure that you are the most prepared version of yourself you can be to achieve optimal results, and I guarantee that if you do the work, you will be exactly that."

The process of doing the work required, however, is extremely hard. Producing feedback on the questions I have asked up to this point and the topics I've encouraged you to reflect on should have been uncomfortable to do. Think again about what I've suggested you implement or remove from your lifestyle; these are not easy decisions to make. But this was all intentional on my part because I recognize your ambition. Your expectations for yourself have already shifted positively from where they were when you picked up this book, and your movement towards realizing your potential is gaining momentum and building speed. The gap that was there at the beginning is closing between your expectations and your potential.

ALWAYS LEAD WITH INTENTION

In the same way that I have encouraged clients and athletes over the years to jump into the resistance, I relish telling clients in consultations how I plan to insert myself into the gap between expectations and potential. One of the easiest things to do in life is to discover what you want to achieve. One of the hardest things in life is to hold yourself accountable to realizing it. The ambition we have towards our goals and potential is nothing more than a dream if we are not willing and able to take steps towards it – steps of intent. Intentionality is the number one factor influencing whether I have seen potential realized or not, even more so than action.

I have read every argument over the years about "what are intentions without actions?" The implication being that action is the key. Don't get me wrong, it is *almost* as important. I am in no way devaluing the importance of action. The fact is, when you work with or coach large teams you see actions going on all around you. Efforts are being made. Brains are working. Interaction is taking place. Sweat is dripping. Yet, you can always, always tell those that are there with intention and those that are just there because they were expected to be there. If you want to shock the gap between expectation and potential you better get in there with a stick of dynamite labeled "intention."

THE INTENTIONAL ATHLETE

The world of sports is the ideal place to highlight the impact of intention. One of my earliest interviews on the podcast was with a former baseball player at LSU turned highly successful financial investor for his company, Horizon Financial Group, Pete Bush. Pete has a reputation in the financial sector for being personally invested in building authentic relationships to help in the growth of people's lives. As of 2022, in addition to being the CEO of a highly successful wealth management company, he is on several committees for the broker-dealer company Cetera Financial Group. But it was back during his time playing at LSU under Hall-of-Fame coach Skip Bertman where he discovered the impact you can have on people by embodying the right intentions while pursuing optimal performance.

Pete was the captain of the first team Skip ever took to the College World Series as the head coach of Louisiana State University. This was a team with a clear identity and a rock-solid core community, and one that had embraced their true value to get to this point. It was all intentional, and the habits of this team were strong enough to bring a first college World Series title to LSU. But they didn't. The championship was not to be theirs that week. And like the majority of most college athletes, Pete finished his career falling short of the ultimate team prize. Like I said at the outset of the chapter, no guarantees.

Realization Exercise

Examine your process for intention.

⇨ Where in your process is intention most noticeable?

⇨ What is it about that part of your process that creates such intention?

⇨ How can you better incorporate intention in your plans ahead and remain mindful of it?

Pete will tell you the team was as ready and prepared as it could be. Their process was filled with the right intentions, and the proof of that would come two years later when LSU returned to the College World Series to win the whole thing. He got to watch the fruits of his labor and help build the championship mindset required in a process toward becoming a championship team. He was not on the pile of players celebrating when the last out was achieved, but he sure contributed to the moment. Because the intention of Coach Skip Bertman was to build a championship *program*, that was the optimal potential he saw at LSU. And championship programs will be the launch pad for championship teams (Bertman's LSU teams made 11 trips to the College World Series over an 18-year career with the school, winning 5 national championships in the process). Players and staff who joined this team understood the intentions required to realize its potential.

While Pete's personal baseball story didn't come with the result he wanted, he recognized the role he played in the long-term shaping of the success of the program. But the Hall-of-Fame football player Steve Atwater not only helped build the foundation of the Denver Broncos teams he played for, but he also reaped the rewards as well. In the National Football League, Steve was a two-time Superbowl champion (1997 and 1998) and eight-time Pro Bowl selection before being named to the Pro Football Hall of Fame class of 2020. When I interviewed Steve, he had recently found out he would be inducted into the Hall of Fame, which is the highest personal honor for any player in the NFL. As much as his statistics made him worthy of consideration and induction into the Hall of Fame, it was his two Super Bowl championships that cemented this man's intentions toward optimal performance.

The team component of football is unlike any other sport out there. Fifty-three-man squads suit up on game day with another 14 players around the team each week to help them practice and prepare for games. What an individual does with their time, their presence, their voice, and their actions are directly influenced by their intentions. In Steve's case, he knew the value he could bring to the team he was on—physically, vocally, and emotionally. Because he knew and accepted his most authentic self (there's that identity from chapter 1 again), he was able to determine how he could impact this team in a winning way. As a player on the field and a leader in the locker room, Steve knew his role and responsibilities and he served them daily. As he referenced in our discussion, many other players sang from the same hymn sheet as he. His teammates brought their best and most authentic selves every day too. So, when their coach Mike Shanahan mapped out his intentions for them to be Super Bowl champions, the player's intentions were assessed and held to the same standard both by coaches and by one another.

The reason I chose to tell both of these competitors' stories is not just because they are great stories, and not just because they played roles in their respective team's journey to eventually *shock the world* and become champions. The common denominator here was value. The value they placed on what they were trying to achieve influenced the intentions they brought to the cause. This, in turn, shaped the value they placed on themselves, which of course would raise their intentions even more as they recognized the role they could each play in realizing their team's potential.

Realization Exercise

Assess the value you place on what you are trying to achieve through this book.

⇨ What does realizing your potential truly mean to you?

⇨ How can you revisit the intentions you have, and build on them knowing this value you have?

⇨ How can you optimize the role you play in this process towards realizing your potential?

DON'T LET THE SIZE OF IT INTIMIDATE YOU

While this has been a very sports themed chapter so far, understand that the very intentional acts these men utilized in the pursuit of optimal sports performance are transferable into any competitive arena. Pete's story of entrepreneurship and finance you already know. Steve, today, is utilizing the very same methods in his role as manager of fan development with the Denver Broncos by connecting the mission of the organization with those who support it the most. If you believe in your potential and you are ambitious enough to go and reveal it, now is the time to lay out the intentions you need within your process. You have educated yourself on the mindset required and are working on implementing it. You are integrating and becoming more familiar with the habits you will need to trust. Now you must inject a level of intentionality into your process to shock the gap between current expectations and realizing potential.

Are your expectations for what you are doing and capable of high enough? Is your perspective of potential clear and accurate? If not, then your ambition will be limited. So often when I tell clients about the gap between their expectations and their potential, I emphasize that it tends to be wider than they realize. Not in a negative way, but more to get them to realize the reason they have yet to optimize their potential is that their current expectations are not as intentional as they thought (and therefore lower than they should be). Furthermore, in time we reveal that they might have been selling themselves short on their true potential (and therefore it is higher than they thought).

It is why I insert myself into the gap as a coach, and why I want to help you insert yourself into your gap right now. Challenge the expectations you have for yourself, especially now that your self-value should be as high as it has ever been. You know you can handle the expectation so demand it of yourself, raise the bar, and insist upon intentions that make you uncomfortable every day. And remember, you bought this book to *shock the world*. Not to wave at the world, not to hang out with the world—to shock it! Now is the time to recognize your potential and establish what is required from your intentions to get there. Even people most of us would consider to be established successes are still looking to challenge the ceiling that is their potential.

IT IS NO LONGER JUST SOMETHING I WANT

I describe the evolution of being ready for coaching as follows.

- Those who need coaching (which in my opinion is just about everyone).

- Those who want coaching (which in my experience is about a third of people).

- Those who HAVE A NEED to be coached (a very small and separate group from the rest).

I'm at a point in my career where I won't just coach anyone; they must at least *want* to be coached. Life gives people enough intel for them to recognize they need coaching, but it's on the individual to shift their mindset towards wanting to be coached. Therefore, those who want coaching are receptive to insights, are professional in the coaching relationship, and consistently see benefits from the journey. But the ones who truly *have* a need to be coached, well that is where the real impact is felt and seen. They seek insight. They *demand* accountability. They initiate communication. They take complete responsibility for their part of the competitive collaboration that should be present when being coached.

Like so many examples I have already provided, the intensity and energy a client or athlete creates through their need for coaching is infectious to me. It creates reciprocal energy that demands that I, as a coach, bring my very best to the table. This extra energy and engagement is all too often incorrectly perceived by teammates or bystanders as favoritism. But a huge element of this perceived "extra attention" that gets overlooked is the element of *accountability*.

I proposed a question one time to an athlete who had complained to me that they felt I was favoring another athlete: "Are you both willing and able to be held accountable daily?" While they looked at me in confusion, no doubt assuming they already were being held to the highest standard of accountability, I explained further. While most of the athletes would disappear quickly after practice, this individual I apparently favored would initiate conversations with me and ask for honest feedback on how they did. Their performance was not always pretty. But because of how good they wanted to be, I held them to a higher standard, so I was consistently challenging them privately to demand more of themselves. From afar, it looks like I'm giving someone extra attention; but the reality is this is an athlete who chose to embrace added responsibility that few around them did. The athlete who made that initial complaint received the challenge I set for them well, and grew because of it. The other athlete, who was already holding himself accountable, ended up qualifying for the 2020 US Olympic team.

Reinvent and Recharge

When I first established myself as a performance coach for business owners, leaders, and those with high ambition, my first client was not exactly what I was envisioning. Bill Whittle, 72 years old, of the insurance company Primerica, committed to becoming a client of mine. You read that right – 72 years old. A guy exactly twice my age saw me as the answer to how he could remain relevant and competitive.

Make no mistake, this was not some guy hanging on to the hope of "still making it." Bill is responsible for one of the largest territories in Primerica's history. He is responsible for the recruitment and training of literally thousands of professionals that have gone on to make successful careers (and impressive bank accounts) for themselves in the process. But when you start your career in your early thirties as Bill did, and remain hungry to progress and improve forty years later, you are acknowledging the need to evolve, change, or replace parts of your process. This proven competitor is heading into his fifth decade of business and still *has* the *need* to make things happen. Hence, when someone like Bill recognizes that he needs help with that process, he gets a coach.

Known as "coach" himself (and as the co-author of "Coachable: Beyond Winning Teams to Changing Lives"), Bill's business success relies on the performance and development of those he is responsible for. When we met in December of 2021, he sensed a growing gap between what he was able to implement and the potential he felt there was in his business. The world had changed, and what was relevant just two years earlier (pre-Covid) was no longer. Bill was even concerned that it could be him who may no longer be relevant. My task as his newly-hired coach was to help him see that not only was he still capable of being relevant, but his already highly effective leadership, recruiting, and training methods just needed to evolve.

Think back to the last process-themed chapter on truth. Bill took initiative at 72 years of age to uncover truths about his process. And in doing so, I was able to introduce him to the gap in his process we could plunge into headfirst. We examined truths and made recurring shocks to the gap in such ways that the process received the reinventions and recharges necessary to enhance Bill's relevance. While I strive to retire by 62, never mind 72, I remain in awe of working with a man looking to shock the gap at such an age. It's a legacy that few others will ever have, and I consider myself privileged to be a part of it as I write these words. So, if a guy in his seventies with enough reasons in his bank account to have retired a decade ago is still eager to shock the gap, what are *you* waiting for?

Realization Exercise

Examine the choices you can make within your process to facilitate personal growth.

⇨ What strengths in your mindset might need to evolve?

⇨ What intention(s) can you introduce into your process to prompt this evolution?

⇨ How will such intention(s) serve you 12 months from now?

RIDE THE GAP

Much like a mountain biker will deal with slopes, bumps, jumps, climbs, and falls when taking on a course, navigating the gap is very much the same. It is not a gap in the sense of a void, it is a gap in the sense of a distance, a distance which is unknown and will only be revealed when—you guessed it—we insert ourselves into it. Brian Lopes is regarded as one of the greatest of all time in the mountain biking world and much like other action sports greats (think Tony Hawk, Kelly Slater, etc.), the guy doesn't feel age is a reason to slow down. Once labeled "undisputedly the best all-around world-class cycling athlete" by USA Today, Brian is a four-time UCI Mountain Bike World Champion and has simply made a career of competing with the world's best.

When you consider Brian's story, you can understand what makes this a process-oriented focus versus an action. The desire to find new ways to challenge yourself is born out of the intention to do so. Brian shared with me that the only approach he has ever had towards life is to find new ways to challenge himself, and this has served him first and foremost on his bike and also in his business endeavors. When he reached new performance standards for riding his bike around a course, his intentions would evolve. He would set his intentions to discover greater, more advanced courses and embrace the process required to take on and master the new challenge. When he formulated his ideas on how to get into the business and entrepreneurial space, his intentions evolved. He strived to learn more about the markets and stakeholders he was trying to reach and surrounded himself with the right people to make it happen.

Whether you are an athlete, an entrepreneur, a leader, a business professional, or someone just ready to follow their potential, you can always aspire towards higher standards. An athlete, entrepreneur, and business person like Brian Lopes doesn't have to strive towards ceilings and potential the way he does, but he chooses to do so anyway. In the same way, you did not have to pick up this book, and I assume no one told you that you have to shock the world. But here you are. You chose this. You are sensing now how guys like Brian and Bill don't do certain things because they just want to; they believe they need to do it in order to feel alive and recognize their truest, most competitive self.

All the people I have referenced so far in this book value themselves and their potential so much that their ambition doesn't dwindle. That recognition of ambition and high value for themselves helps define their intentions and fuels their processes. This can be you and this will be you. Truly committing to your potential will provide the commitment required to fully prepare you for executing optimal performance. That is my guarantee.

You are ready to Shock the Gap because

⇨ You are willing to accept the gap is bigger than you thought and are intentional about closing it.

⇨ You value what you are trying to accomplish and the investment required to achieve it.

⇨ You embrace the need to evolve your process and intentions to keep closing the gap.

Why we should Shock the Gap

| Embrace Expectations | Embrace Potential | Embrace Process | Embrace Success |

SHOCK
THE EXECUTION

ACTION STEP

The deliberate nature of the work we have done has brought us to this point (insert your favorite hype music here … slowly fade it in). Everything you have done up to here has been through choice, and you didn't come this far to get cold feet now. Committing to optimal performance is the final part of this journey, and the word *commitment* to me has always had an absolute connotation to it. The same way I have always been able to detect those with and without intent in the process, I've always been able to tell a committed action from one without it. Commitments rarely work out when someone doesn't comprehend what they are committing to, and when you have done the work that you have done, there cannot be much left to clarify. I intended to prepare you for the moment, now it is up to you to go execute (blast the hype music!).

We have spent eight chapters shocking our internal systems, processes, relationships, intentions, and many other elements to bring us to this point. The eight shocks that have formed the framework of this book and this moment, have made us ready to execute. They justify the fact that we have pursued a passion and a potential we see within ourselves that we want the world to be witness to. Now it is up to us to reveal our optimal self and optimal performance through execution.

I chose the word *execution* very deliberately for this penultimate chapter. Execution is carrying out or putting into effect a plan, order, or course of action. Based on this definition, can you see how the work you have done up to this point has ensured you are ready to do exactly that? Put the work you have done into effect! It is your duty to yourself to do so. There is nothing to reconsider. There is nothing left to renegotiate.

Is there? Nope, nothing left at all. I'm willing to raise the stakes a little actually and suggest that you have not simply prepared for this moment to execute, you have brought this moment into existence.

It Will Manifest If You Do the Rest

Speaking things into existence is considered to be a truly powerful technique. But it is not a wish so much as it is a statement of intent; and in the case of this chapter, bringing a statement like this to fruition comes in the form of executing. I have always been a prolific believer in this—communicating with athletes what they are capable of, encouraging clients to think big—and I have had this approach reaffirmed by many guests on the podcast. But my respect for this is so great that it has led me to always consider what I believe can be accomplished before actually stating it. We don't shock the world by simply wandering around identifying things that we want. But we can make significant and life-altering achievements come to fruition by understanding and embracing the commitment to follow through and execute on what we want.

When I met Amy Thompson in the summer of 2020 she was dealing with a lot. Amy was and is a self-made woman who made a name for herself within a field that did not necessarily offer many opportunities for female leadership. Amy is the owner and CEO of IDEA Health & Fitness, a guiding force in the health, fitness, and nutrition industry since 1982. During my interview with her in 2020, she shared how she had gotten to where she was on the principles she frequently shared with others and lived by. In doing so, she was consistently fueling her intentions for the future as well. She was a tried and tested practitioner in the act of manifesting, and she was speaking things into existence back in 2020 that she would achieve two years later. For Amy was the Vice President and General Manager when I first interviewed her, and when she was appointed owner and CEO of IDEA two years later, I simply had to bring her back on the show.

Without execution, a moment like one Amy was striving towards could not manifest itself. It is not an act of declaration one time and then waiting to see what happens. Amy stated her goal clearly and consistently enough that she created the necessary accountability to fuel every action ahead of her. Personal growth, truths, relationships, habits, and gaps could all be assessed, worked on, and embraced to validate that she would be able to execute and attain what she set out to. Becoming a female CEO of a global health and fitness brand is a resounding shock to the fitness and business world. There would have been plenty of times along the way where Amy could have moved aside or accepted less, not ruffled feathers or messed with the status quo. But this was her life purpose; she knew she could do it and made it happen.

Realization Exercise

Consider something you would like to see manifest into reality.

⇨ What element of realism is there within that goal to prompt action?

⇨ How accountable are you willing to hold yourself and those around you to making it happen?

⇨ What would it mean to you to see this come to fruition?

So, what have you done to prove to yourself that you are ready? If you have to, now would be a good time to go back and look over the notes you have written, plans you have made, steps you have laid out, and maybe even some action already taken. The work you have done is a validation of your readiness and the confirmation you need that it is time to roll this thing out for the world to see. This does not have to be the final product or performance, because in many ways, this is just the beginning. Like any athlete trying out for a team, any performer auditioning for a part, any entrepreneur presenting a prototype, or any other first-time moments, now is the time to just get in front of people. Initiate action and assess the quality of it. Go show someone what you have been working on. Go get a feeling of what it is like to make something happen.

PRACTICE WHAT YOU PLAN TO DO

Performing *before* the performance is another way to look at this, a dress rehearsal if you will. In sports this is better known as practice; at least that's how I've always viewed it. The term *practice* is one of those words that has lost its meaning somewhat over time concerning training and preparation. Knowing that all sports lead to some form of assessed performance makes for a good reason to practice that performance. In my experience, however, the practice has become as much about simply working hard as it has about *preparing to perform*. Shifting a perspective towards preparing to perform can open your eyes to embracing execution more frequently. If you practice performing, you are preparing to execute. You are embracing what will be expected of you when it comes to delivering on your high expectations to realize your potential.

Three days before Brooks swam his 100 meters freestyle at the 2020 Olympic trials, we prepared to perform with some race rehearsal work. It was awful. I am usually not so extreme in my assessments, but considering what we were there to accomplish, awful does it justice. His technique was out of sorts, he showed no aggression in his speed, and there was no sign of an athlete ready to *shock the world*. But that did not mean he was not ready to do exactly that in three days, it just meant we needed to review a couple of things about his pre-race routine.

Despite the exercise at hand being a race rehearsal, we both agreed he did not use the hour before the exercise the way he needed to in order to optimize the performance. It exposed the big truth in his process that needed to be exposed; this was not just going to happen. Optimal performances are deliberate acts and efforts. So much of this book is about preparing you to shock the world, but as we approach the final pages of the book, this is the time where a more deliberate focus is paramount. Make things happen. Deliver on your intentions.

Embrace Everything That Comes with It

The reality of the situation is another component to consider here as well. When we build up goals and monumental moments we are trying to achieve, we can sometimes disconnect our goals from our reality. Not in the sense of having an unrealistic goal, but more of not accepting that the moment is coming, that it is time to deliver on our efforts. The reality is that if you plan to *shock the world*, you embrace the very reality of executing under pressure and expectation.

However unlikely or unrealistic your goals might seem to those in the world you plan to shock, you believe otherwise. You believe you are simply realizing the potential of yourself, of your work, or maybe of your product. Embrace the need to execute. Be deliberate with your efforts in preparing to perform. In the case of Brooks and his race rehearsal exercise, it was one final slap in the face he needed to embrace the reality that we were at the competition. It was soon to be *now or never* and he had to be the one who executed a world-shocking performance.

Realization Exercise

Consider the way in which you will execute and be assessed.

⇨ How are you making time to practice and prepare for that moment?

⇨ How will you assess the extent of your ability to execute before there is more at stake?

⇨ How can you deliberately establish confirmation that your time has come and you are ready?

Enough of the Waiting

When it comes to slaps in the face and finding out the hard way if you are ready, few of life's ventures serve such moments as consistently as owning your own business. As I have started my venture into entrepreneurship, I have been spoiled by the amount of support I have received, but even more fortunate to learn from those that have been there and done it.

Having always considered myself a pupil in the school of trial and error, I have consistently told athletes and clients that we can try something out knowing it may fail. I was so excited to discover so many stories of failures and lessons learned from my ever-growing new network. Time and time again, these smart, successful, and highly-regarded professionals shared tales of falling flat on their faces despite being so sure they were ready. But they consistently shared a common takeaway when they looked back and relived such times in their journey.

"Had I never just tried and put myself out there, I would never have gotten to where I am today."

My now good friend Jack Karavich came into my entrepreneur world as I was just getting started. He is a tried and tested student of the good and bad ideas, the good and bad business practices, and the plenty of ugly stuff in and around the world of entrepreneurship too. He just so happened to have landed on an absolute diamond of an idea a year before we met, which he named Tigeraire and which has become its own product line and industry.

There is simply nothing like it out there. It is a cooling airflow device for football helmets and industrial hard hats that keeps the head significantly cooler to limit problems like dehydration, fatigue, and sub-optimal performance. I can confidently say that no matter when you are reading this, Tigeraire is more successful now than it was when I wrote this chapter, and that trend will only continue.

When I convinced Jack to come on the podcast and explain how ideas are brought to life, he spoke my language and kept the message simple. "Make it happen and get in front of people." Why? Feedback! A guy like Jack doesn't always even schedule his opportunities to get feedback; he has his product in the trunk of his car for when he sees a target consumer (picture a sweaty, exhausted-looking worker on a building site). He wanders up and asks if they'd like to try something on and just like that he has more feedback and probably a new customer as well.

Realization Exercise

Identify opportunities where you can get in front of people.

⇨ What type of scenarios can you prepare for before they even present themselves?

⇨ How can you ensure that you capitalize on such scenarios and get the feedback you need?

⇨ How is each moment of execution guiding you towards your ultimate goal?

Be Deliberate and Do It

I do not doubt the journey I have taken you on in this book has served you realizing your potential accordingly, but the beauty of getting to this point is that you can receive feedback. Go and execute and get some feedback. Are you onto something? Are there parts you need to go back and rethink? Is it possible you missed something obvious? Are you closer than you even realized to the big moment? How close are you?

What a guy like Jack is doing involves deliberate acts on deliberate acts, each a moment of execution where he is carrying out or putting into effect a plan, order, or course of action. There are simply so many ways we can execute each and every day to get the feedback we desire, but only if we are willing to put ourselves out there. Whether opportunities present themselves is up to you. A moment of execution stems from your core foundation of identity. Everything that has grown between planting the seeds of this foundation to the moment of execution has involved many deliberate acts. Now is the time to be as deliberate as you can possibly be.

Shocking the execution is as much about you as it is about the performance, the product, or the result you aspire to deliver. Are you ready to shock the world? Because if you cannot handle the concept of executing, then this world of yours will have to wait. You did not stumble and land on this page; you worked your way to here. At this point, it is time to assess and reveal how and why you are the person to *shock the world*.

You are ready to Shock the Execution because

⇨ You understand the expectations of manifesting and will speak what you are willing to do.

⇨ You are willing to practice performing to remain connected to the reality of the situation.

⇨ You deliberately create opportunities to assess where you are in your preparations.

Why we should Shock the Execution

> Create Opportunity > Create Feedback > Create Expectations > Create Success

SHOCK
THE WORLD

It's a feeling unlike any other.

Even now when I look back on it, I find myself grinning to myself at the fact that we went and pulled off the shock. Just seconds after Brooks reached for the wall and claimed the fourth and final automatic relay spot for the US 4x100 meters freestyle relay by three one-hundredths of a second (I knew he had it), I was flying down a flight of stairs so fast I was practically falling. Brooks emerged from the pool right in front of me and I motioned to him to get over here. "Shock the world!" was all he heard me scream into his ear for the next few seconds. Then a few expletives. Then a few "Love you man, proud of you brother" before I let him go from my grip to go take care of media stuff. It's an indescribable feeling when you witness potential being realized. Yes, this was on a huge stage and it truly altered an athlete's entire career; but for me, in so many ways, I had experienced this feeling before.

As I have noted already, this was always my coaching philosophy: to help people realize their potential. Not swimmers, not athletes—people. While I can proudly look back on how the seeds of this book were planted and how the title represents a truly life-changing and forever impactful journey I was privileged to be a part of, I am equally proud of the many shock the world moments that came before this that I had a hand in, and the many I continue to witness and benefit from being a part of.

Brooks Curry
In His Words

The Shock the World Journey

I will never forget sitting down in your office for the first time and telling you that I wanted to go to the Olympic Games. Your message of how so many other people had sat in this chair and made similar comments but not done what was necessary stuck with me. It shaped the mindset I knew I had to show up to practice with every day from that moment onwards. Even the smallest details like the color swim cap I wore. You told me when I wore the black cap for practice that it's a cap people wear when they mean business. So, I chose to wear it daily because I wanted to mean business daily.

When we first started working towards the goal it was all about figuring out what I could control and was able to change to start the process. It was a goal that appeared so far away at first and by simply figuring out what I needed to incorporate into my process and habits, we were able to create the steps that aligned with the goal, which helped so much in those first few months.

I became comfortable with what was required of me. I started to see myself doing things in practice that matched up with some of the things the top 10 guys in the US were doing. By the time we got to the spring of 2021 it was no longer about knowing it could be done, but more about seeing it all the way through. The structure of the 27-day training phase, for example, allowed for the environment and routine I needed to show up and perform to elite standards every day I was asked to. I became truly comfortable with what would be required of me.

Just because I was trying to shock the world did not make it any less shocking to me when I saw I had finished in the top four. I was so shocked! But the composure we kept in those few days once we arrived at Olympic Trials helped a lot. I was an underdog, no one expected anything of me, which allowed me to focus on myself. But I also knew I had one shot. There was no reason to think of it any other way. I knew what was expected of me, and by the time I was swimming the last 25 meters I knew I was close. But like I said, seeing that I had done it ... So shocked!

I believe that we all owe it to ourselves to try and realize our potential. I recall thinking early on in my swimming career why not try and become the best swimmer in the world? It seems like something a lot of people might say, but I was never afraid of that thought or to go after the goal. While I am still working on that specific goal, it made discussing going to the Olympics very similar. Why not me? I want to do it and I believe I can. Why not just go do it? The goal might seem far out there right now, but you have to start somewhere. Embrace the fact you are doing something that you or maybe no one has ever done before. Commit to the work. Believe in your potential.

"I truly could not have this without you. From the moment I told you my goals in your office, I know it would be possible through you. You have allowed me to achieve my dreams, and I am forever grateful. Thank you, thank you, thank you so much."

- Project Shock the World, **Brooks Curry**

It Won't Always Be a Shock

For every one shock-worthy performance, there are always a few almost shocks and lost shocks in there as well. So often that is the part of these books that the author won't cover—the misses. Sometimes despite people walking the walk, it just doesn't quite come to fruition the way they anticipated. Like I said a couple of chapters ago, nothing about the result here is guaranteed. But the residual effects of the nine chapters and shocks I have mapped out to this point will impact many more moments to come.

The reality is, life is short and we cannot be sure what tomorrow will bring, so what better time to act than now? I have, however, witnessed many individuals get very close to a moment where they seem destined to realize their potential, only to fall short in an immediate sense, and then shock another world further down the road. My point is, that you will shock the world. Maybe not today, and maybe not the first time you try, but your choice to follow the steps outlined in this book leaves you destined to do so eventually.

Moreover, despite a deliberate focus on a specific world you plan to shock, you might just end up shocking yourself in how you end up realizing your potential. That is the beauty of this book; while you arm yourself by developing the inner growth, processes, and actions necessary to shock one world, you are advancing your potential in areas you may never have considered.

You Never Know

Clients come to me consistently emphasizing a particular focus they feel they need to work on and develop in. And while I always honor such requests and set out to deliver on them, I tell them, "Stay open-minded to other areas of growth you hadn't even considered, for we don't know what we don't know." When a client starts working with me, they are getting a specific influence on their life for the first time—me! This is not my way of elevating my stature in some egotistical way, it is just a truth. They have never worked me in this capacity before, so they will receive guidance and perspectives at times that are new to them.

Renewed perspectives and fresh insights can serve as catalysts for thought that would otherwise never have been pursued. And just like that, a client can find themselves exposed to potential in themselves they were never aware of. Maybe they are drawn to exploring such potential further. Maybe they decide to embark on a new path with new focuses. Before long, maybe they just go and shock that world.

As I first introduced back in chapter three and explored further in chapter eight, by now I am hopeful you understand what it means to have a need to do what it is you are setting out to do. While it is an approach that will serve you in closing the gap between current expectations and your true potential, it will keep you open-minded towards new ways that you can realize your potential as well. Realizing potential is my profession, and I believe it can become yours too. While I focus on many others when it comes to doing exactly this, I believe you are ready to facilitate this process in yourself, at least to start.

SEE IT ALL THE WAY THROUGH

Consider yourself firmly rooted at the center of the universe that is your life and know you have control over what you welcome into that space and what you don't. While you strive to perform or produce in a way to shock a particular world, know that after the first, second, and potentially many more moments of execution, you will be better for having gone through it. You will continue to look around your life and see evidence of new skills, challenges overcome, opportunities created, connections made, and strength acquired towards realizing your potential yet again. And as your universe strengthens and grows, so do you. You start to notice just how great your potential truly is. You feel incentivized to keep going no matter what. You strive towards and thrive upon discovering more about what you are truly capable of.

Every story that I shared of guests that have joined me on the Career Competitor podcast has a common theme. They saw their quest to realize their potential through to the end, and in some cases continue to pursue it today. The grit that comes with this is a trait in itself that is hard to find and could have easily been a chapter in this book. It embodies the more obvious traits of an extremely hardworking mindset and professionalism towards performance. But the most impactful component of an individual embodying grit is a unique belief that they must realize their potential and finish what they started. As competitors, they refuse to be derailed by countless distractions along the way. They believe their destiny is to realize their potential, and there is nothing and no one capable of convincing them otherwise.

Does the notion of you *not* shocking the world that you set out to deflate you in any way? I empathize with you if it does. I have been there and more than likely will be back there again. The beauty, however, of what my journey has proven to me time and time again, is that as long as you remain loyal to a growth mindset, there will be a step forward coming again soon.

Stopping and accepting you are not capable would be a disservice to the work done in this book. As the saying goes, "Where one door closes, another door opens." That is what this book has instilled in you: the ability to find and open other doors.

Anyone who has worked closely with me will tell you how much I cannot stand watching potential go to waste. It hurts me at my core in a way that stings and that stays with me. I do not want that for you. And trust me when I say that you don't want that for you either. Hopefully, this book will ensure that fewer people let their potential go unrealized, and I know I can count on you to do your part in making sure that happens!

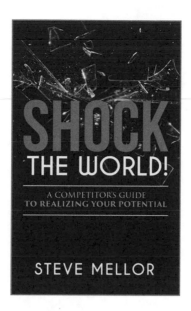

To order additional copies of Shock the World! A Competitors Guide to Realizing Your Potential go to:

If you would like more information regarding bulk book orders of Shock the World! A Competitors Guide to Realizing Your Potential, please connect directly with Steve at Steve@careercompetitor.com

Author, Steve Mellor is offering tailored services in association with this book to those looking to further apply the content and grow as competitors.

If you would like more information regarding Keynote opportunities, coaching, and training, please connect directly with

Steve at Steve@careercompetitor.com

ACKNOWLEGEMENTS

I have to start by acknowledging what makes the fact I wrote this book the greatest shock to the world. Throughout my education, my English teachers were no inspiration for me to become a writer. Far from it. Had I allowed their grades to determine my capability, this book never happens. But they told me one thing consistently that I held onto. "You need to stop writing as though you are speaking, this is English literature, not English speaking". How I interpreted that feedback, however, was "find a world where you can write through your voice". Well, sorry to inform you teachers, but that C-average English student of yours went and wrote himself a book (also, thank you to my editor Sean, you caught a few grammatical doozies in there, brother).

I am approaching this in the order of how the book came to fruition, so I have to start with the genesis, Brooks Curry. For as crazy as it was that we achieved what we did, you were the one that got it done. You shocked the world. Throughout the journey from recruiting you, building our relationship, to coaching you, it was a pleasure to watch you grow and become the world-class athlete you are today. While your story is now a part of swimming folklore, our journey will be something I cherish forever. Thank you for allowing me the chance to create history with you.

In addition, the hundreds of athletes I have had the pleasure of swim coaching between 2009 – 2021: athletes from North Carolina State University between 2009 – 2011 and the many athletes I coached and interacted with at LSU from 2011 – 2012 and 2015 – 2021, you all impacted me. My philosophies on life and coaching have come from your willingness to listen to and respect what I had to say. Seeing so many of you grow and succeed from such insight convinced me I had something to share and write about. I always tried to say thank you to every one of you over those years, but for any I missed, consider this your belated thank you.

Dave Geyer, I include you at this point because so many of the principles and insight I offer throughout this book were tried, tested, tried differently, retested, and eventually proven because you allowed for them to be. While in many ways we went through the toughest of situations during our time working together, we grew enormously, and have so many stories we will continue to look back on fondly and cherish for years to come. Above all, thank you for your friendship.

Dr. Denis Cauvier, the man behind the scenes that mentored and coached me through the writing and publication process. You told me I had something worth putting down on the page and that I was capable of being the one that could write it. You promised me a lot and have been a man of your word throughout which has meant the world to me. Thank you for your guidance and support.

To my Career Competitor podcast guests, all 130 of you (and counting), while I wish I could have written a book where I included you all, know that every conversation has impacted me. Each of you found ways to shift my perspective on a topic just enough that it allowed me to continually grow as a coach and a person. It was not an easy task to select just 18 guests to include in the book, but in many ways, you all contributed to the content. You all chose to spend time and talk to a guy that in most cases you did not know, but you spoke with me intending to make an impact on listeners, and for that, I am so grateful.

To my clients, both present and past, I always appreciate the fact that I get paid to do what I do and that many of you appreciate it enough to want to pay me again and again. Realizing potential is what I truly live for, and the competitively collaborative (see what I did there?) environment we create for becoming your optimal self is my true happy place. I hope you enjoyed seeing some of the approaches I take with you sprinkled throughout the book. Thank you for your trust and investment in me.

To my beta readers, Pat Fellows, Jennifer Feduccia, and Bill Whittle. You played an integral part in this process that served my confidence in knowing this book was ready to be released. Thank you for the investment you made for a cause that means so much to me. Your next drink is on me!

To my friends, you know who you are, much like how I address community within this book, you do not need too many people in your circle, you just need to know you have the right ones for you. While I could easily name each one of you, I am only going to single out my best man, Pete Burgham. From being immature kids around the streets and swimming pool of Chester, England, to being immature husbands and fathers today with an ocean between us, you have spent 20 years in my corner making sure I never gave up on my potential. Thank you for being the best friend a guy could ask for.

To you the reader, yes you, thank you for the time and investment you have made in the reading of my book. There will never come a time when I lose an ounce of appreciation for those that choose to listen and pay attention to the insight and guidance I offer. It is why I am so careful about the words I choose and the messages I share; you have been kind enough to pay attention, so I want to return that generosity with impact in any way I can. I hope you look back on this as time well spent.

To my sister, Caroline, the creative one of the family, you have been an artist my entire life and the life you have painted into existence with John, Lizzie, and Thomas proves the message of this book. While you were first unsure of your ability and value, you have shown your world what you are capable of and continue to inspire me as an entrepreneur and family man on what it means to show up in all areas of life.

To my mum and dad, full transparency, you played no part at all in the writing of this book (you both had to know that was coming!). But in all seriousness, not once did you ever get in the way of me trying to realize my potential and become my optimal self. Growing up, you worked to allow Caroline and me to chase our passions. You were always available to ensure we could take advantage of any opportunity available to us, no matter the potential inconvenience it could have caused you. You laid the platform required for your children to have a chance to shock the world.

Finally, my all-day, everyday motivation, my inspiration, and my best friend that I get to call my wife, Britney. The competitor in me conceded defeat in being the lesser half of this relationship the moment I met you. You will forever be my better half. You provided me with our gifts from God in Ella and Jake, and the three of you motivate me to be my optimal self every day. Thanks for letting me escape often enough to write this thing, hopefully, it was enough to make you proud.